STRANGE BUT TRUE, AMERICA

WEIRD TALES FROM ALL 50 STATES

JOHN HAFNOR
AUTHOR

DALE CRAWFORD
ILLUSTRATOR

Lone Pine Productions
Fort Collins, Colorado

Library of Congress Control Number: 2009900497

ISBN+10   0-9648175-5-1
ISBN+13   978-0-9648175-5-5
Manufactured in the United States of America

Published by Lone Pine Productions
Distribution and Marketing: Attn: John Hafnor, Lone Pine Productions
3116 W. County Rd. 38E, Fort Collins, CO 80526
Phone: 970-223-2747   Cell: 970-443-5211   Email: jhafnor@aol.com

Book editor, John Hughes, Fort Collins, CO

Cover and Book Design by NZ Graphics, Denver, CO
Contact Nick Zelinger nzgraphics@qwestoffice.net

Discover unpublished stories and more at **www.StrangeTrueUS.com**

To Ralph, the wind beneath my wings.

~ Dale Crawford

To dear Lori, the finest "second chance" a man ever received.

~ John Hafnor

CONTENTS

Words from the Illustrator

My American History teacher, Mr. Beirne, wrote these words in my high school year book: "History is not always made in history class. Good luck in art." Looking back now, his words were true. Though my first love was always art, I've found a way to combine art and history. My brother was my inspiration in so many ways. Seven years older than me, Ralph suffered from polio, and drawing was one of the many activities he was good at. I am and forever will be in awe of his creativity and spirit.

The handicap didn't stop him from doing what he wanted to do, and going where he wanted to go. When we weren't playing army or cowboys on our farm, we could be found drawing tanks, soldiers, cowboys and Indians. As we grew, his creative interests went on to other things. But mine stayed with drawing. I can't remember a time when I didn't draw. My interest in the American West was heightened by growing up in the 1950s. Back then, the theater in our small town sold summertime punch cards for the Saturday afternoon movies. Every week, we looked forward to multiple cartoons, cliff-hangers, and two feature-length movies. One was usually a Western featuring Roy Rogers or Gene Autry, with side kicks like Gabby Hayes and Smiley Burnette.

When I wasn't watching or playing cowboys, I was drawing them — so it was only natural that when TV came along I continued to love Westerns. By the early 60s, there were more Westerns on TV then today's cornucopia of reality shows … and that's saying a lot. One can trace my growing interest in old photo albums and school pictures — that's me in the fancy cowboy shirt and boots. I still remember the first pair of boots my Dad got for me, and I can still smell the leather. Yup, I was hooked on the American West…or what I thought it was. Later I realized what had drawn me to the story of the settling of our country was not the real history, but the "reel" history of movies and TV. Nevertheless, such exposure motivated me to learn more. My interest in the West and American history has grown hand-in-hand with my chosen profession of art. After art school I entered the world

of commercial graphics, married Fran, and we moved to Milwaukee. For the next few years, I worked at an art studio and then an advertising agency. There I learned my craft, and on the side still drew and painted my beloved Western subject matter.

By 1973, our daughter completed kindergarten and we three moved to Colorado. The trek fulfilled a dream of ours. I knew that my passion for history and the West in general wasn't going to go away — and I felt that my art would sell better in Colorado then it did in the state where the Packers, cheese and beer are king. We felt like pioneers of the past, except that we headed west in a Chevy Nova instead of a covered wagon! In Colorado we found employment, and I met publisher Mike Koury, the owner of Old Army Press. Over the years, Mike introduced me to a number of authors in search of an artist. That's how I met John Hafnor. As some of you know, this is the second book I've had the pleasure to illustrate for John. The first was *Strange But True, Colorado.*

I couldn't have found a better person to work with, and I feel blessed that we had another opportunity to work together on this latest book.

I always felt that I was born 100 years too late. With current technology we still can't physically go back in time — but we can experience the past by simply opening a book. America's history is so rich, varied and vast that you can be assured of finding your area of interest, just as I did. Isn't that part of the reason you picked up this book? Do you realize how young our country is? The last surviving widow of a Civil War veteran died in 2008, having married an older Confederate veteran in her youth.

Of the many books I have illustrated, the Hafnor-authored titles stand out as among the most fun and educational. So as the cowboys of the Old West said: "Tighten your cinch, pull your hat down tight and mount up, partner," because you're about to take a wild ride down some side trails of our nation's history.

Dale Crawford
Fort Collins, Colorado

Words from the Author

For most of us, history can enlighten only if it first entertains. With this as my compass, I began a five-year quest for the 50 strangest American stories — one for each state.

I figured there must be a least one enormously entertaining historical tale from each of our states. I was wrong. There are many such tales from each state. Thus, my biggest job became selecting that *most* compelling tale from your home state … and every state.

I hope you agree with my choices. But in truth I sometimes cheated — for a handful of states I've selected two or even three tales that seemed equally fascinating. For "surplus" tales I assembled a final and potentially most popular chapter: "Thumbing Thru America's Weirdest" is a scrolling map and series of thumbnail accounts of the arcane from each state's "attic." This section is arranged for armchair "travel" across our country, pausing briefly in each state. "Thumbing…" begins on page 129, and is just one example of how this book can be read from back to front, front to back, or one random tale at a time.

I have mostly avoided stories involving ghosts, witchcraft, demons and the supernatural. The reading public has a finite appetite for such topics, but infinite curiosity for stories that at first appear unbelievable yet are ultimately true.

But when pressed, good historians admit that most major events contain inscrutable elements — one example being the Kennedy assassination. Albert Einstein said, "The fairest thing we can experience is the mysterious." Thus, by design you will find lingering mystery in many tales. If such puzzles motivate you to uncover your own new details, so much the better.

In these puzzling tales you will also encounter that gray zone where myth and legend bump up against historical fact. Separating fact from fable is not always a tidy affair, as you'll see in the stories from California, New Hampshire, Arizona and New Mexico.

You'll note many chapter titles read like newspaper headlines. We've also designed the text in newspaper-like columns, edited to Associated Press standards. These are reflections of my early career with the *Rapid City* (SD) *Journal* and the *Stockton* (CA) *Record*.

While at the *Journal* I bumbled and stumbled into the writing of books. I was then penning a modest series of promotional columns on the frontier history of the Black Hills. That's when executives of Falcon Press approached me. They felt the columns might make an attractive little book, if someone would add illustrations and proper editing. Thus was born my 110-page *Black Hills Believables*. For twenty-seven years this slender volume has remained a steady seller in the Black Hills tourist trade.

Then came books with the same formula of brevity, weird history, and copious illustrations: *Strange But True, Colorado, Trekking the Last Badland, Wahres Aus Dem Wilden Westen* for German speakers, and now *Strange But True, America*.

My written words have always been inspired by my late mother, who published her first and only book at age 88. *Looking Back* was her prosaic portrait of the waning homestead days in South Dakota's Badlands. Marian Hafnor Edwards displayed formidable energy and enthusiasm in the publication of *Looking Back*. Her experience, when added to mine, seems to confirm that each of us carries a story within. Marian would have told you that with enough time this story will surely end up on the pages of a book. Your book.

I have lived in Colorado since 1990. My few acres shelter a home located precisely on the margin where pine-scented mountains meet the Great Plains. I imagine that if America were a huge book, this place would be the stitched hinge where eastern and western chapters come together. This also is home to my wife Lori, and our assorted animals. On occasional blessed days we welcome home our remarkable children — Adam Hafnor, Kellie Bonham, Joel Hafnor, Emily Bonham and Andrew Hafnor. Each is now an accomplished young adult, and forever a member of my tribe.

Creative endeavors always owe enormous debt to the tribe of people who believe in the artist. I am no different. This book is dedicated to the named and unnamed who believed in me.

First on this list is my wife, Lori King Bonham Hafnor. Her support has been emotional but also practical. Lori edited each tale from a reader's perspective, and offered many positive suggestions. She labored on the indexing and fact-checking. I also owe that deep debt which can never be repaid to my siblings Mary, Cam and Tom. The same can be said of my stalwart friends Scott Ashbaugh,

Ross Spalding, Steve Meyer and John Hughes.

Finally, I must mention a great professional joy of my life — the opportunity to co-create books with illustrator Dale Crawford.

Crawford's evocative pen blended so well with the written word that he is not simply "the illustrator" of *Strange But True, America,* but my full partner in this project. See more of his artwork, and indeed many unpublished tales that nearly made it into this book, by visiting our website at www.StrangeTrueUS.com.

To quote Lord Byron, "Truth is always strange; stranger than fiction." See if you don't agree as you page through these splinters of the American cross.

John Hafnor
Fort Collins, Colorado

'BAMA Einstein Born into Slavery

What if an Einstein-like genius was born to slavery on a Southern plantation, with no chance to learn reading and writing? It happened in 1849 in Jefferson County, Alabama with the humble birth of Andrew Jackson Beard. Emancipated during the Civil War, 15-year-old Andrew worked at what he knew best: sharecropping. But things changed after a trip to Montgomery, Ala. by ox cart to sell 50 bushels of apples. "It took me three weeks to make that trip," he later observed. "I quit farming after that."

Instead, Beard built and operated a prosperous flour mill in Hardwicks, Ala. In Hardwicks, Beard's brilliant mechanical mind blossomed with the invention of a double plow — the first of many patents for the inventor. He sold his plow design for $4,000. Another plow patent followed, garnering $5,200. The illiterate Beard used these profits to launch a new career as a successful real estate capitalist. He was on his way to becoming one of the Deep South's first African-American millionaires. His inventive mind never stopped churning out bright new ideas, and by 1890 Beard had perfected and patented a rotary steam engine.

Because he could neither read nor write, Beard signed the rotary engine patent (indeed, all his patents) with a simple "X." Historians still ponder what mental gifts may have remained hidden because Beard was denied a basic education by slavery.

Soon Beard's mechanical abilities were in high demand, prompting offers of employment as a carpenter, then a blacksmith, then fatefully as an employee of the Alabama & Chattanooga Railroad.

Railroads were America's biggest business, and one of the most dangerous places to work. In those days, coupling cars together was a highly hazardous operation requiring a rail worker to brace himself between cars and drop a metal pin into place at the exact moment the cars came together.

Few railroad men kept all their fingers. Many lost arms and hands. Others were caught between cars and crushed to death during coupling. Andrew Beard witnessed such tragedies, and they sparked his great epiphany. He sat down to sketch the brilliant invention he called the "Jenny Coupler," which could secure cars automatically by merely bumping them together. His invention revolutionized the railroad industry while saving countless limbs and lives.

Near the turn-of- the-century, Andrew Jackson Beard signed over his coupler company and patent. He left with a check for $50,000, then a small fortune.

Those who saw Beard walk away with the check noticed his pronounced limp. That was fine with him, because for Beard it was always more about the limp and less about the money. As an employee of the Alabama & Chattanooga Railroad, Beard himself lost a leg in a brutal coupling accident.

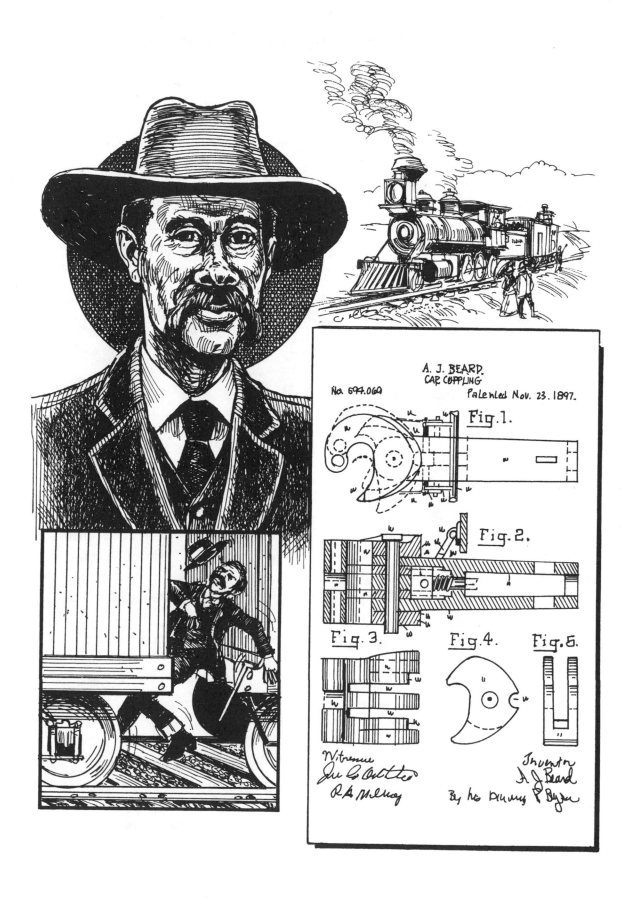

Polar Crater Strikes Terror

Alaska is home to 40 active volcanoes — more than any state. The Last Frontier state also claims the greatest volcanic event of the 20th century. The year was 1912 … and the eruption of Novarupta was 10 times more powerful than Mount St. Helens.

Novarupta's ash cloud, towering 20 miles, was visible from much of Alaska. This same ash cloud would reach Africa 10 days later. Sitka-by-the-Sea residents, 750 miles to the east, were startled by the blast's noise, which took one hour to reach them.

Sitka has its own volcano. Imposing but dormant, Mount Edgecumbe rises 3,200 feet above Sitka and is the namesake of local Mt. Edgecumbe High School.

Sitka, Alaska's "First City," was discovered in 1741 by Russia's Vitus Bering, namesake of the Bering Sea. Sitka became the capital of Russian Alaska. And it was in Sitka in 1867 that Russia formally ceded Alaska to the United States at the stupendous price of less than 2 cents per acre!

Few know the real story behind the sale. For decades Russia reaped enormous profits from sea otter furs, and then proceeded to hunt otters to near extinction. With that lucrative trade gone, Russia was eager to offload the considerable expense of maintaining its colony. Enter U.S. Secretary of State William Seward.

Critics called the purchase Seward's Folly, but soon it was recognized as history's greatest real estate bargain. Yet for years the total American presence in vast Alaska was a single customs agent stationed in the capital of Sitka.

More than 100 years later the unthinkable happened when terrified Sitka residents spilled out of their homes to gaze up at Mount Edgecumbe — the crater was spewing thick black smoke. Soon neighbor was asking neighbor, "Is our volcano active again? Will it erupt?" Phones at the radio and police stations were ringing off the hook.

The smoke turned out to be the work of 51-year-old Porky Bickar, Sitka's legendary prankster. Bickar had arranged for a local chopper to drop 210 old tires and assorted smoke bombs into the crater, whereupon Porky himself soaked the pile with diesel fuel — and lit a match.

Alaska Airlines Vice President Jimmy Johnson heard about Mount Edgecumbe's activity, and instructed his pilots to fly over the crater to give passengers a bird's eye view. The Associated Press carried the news worldwide.

This wasn't Porky's only prank (he once entered a Lady Godiva look-alike in Sitka's annual parade). But it was his best. There was one problem though: Porky notified the FAA and local police ahead of time, but forgot to alert the Coast Guard. The regional Coast Guard commander sent a cutter to investigate, and then ordered a helicopter to take a closer look. The chopper pilot radioed back that all he saw was burning tires … and "April Fool" painted in the snow.

Porky Bickar had perpetrated what many call the best April Fool's prank ever. The spoof was so imprinted in the local psyche that when Mount St. Helens erupted years later, a resident wrote Bickar an angry letter saying, "This time you've gone too far!"

Rogue Camels Haunt the Southwest

America's grand experiment with camels began in Texas, but ended in Arizona.

Back in 1856, Secretary of War Jefferson Davis was convinced that camels would be superior mounts for soldiers crossing America's arid Southwest. That year, the first shipment of Egyptian camels arrived in Texas.

Davis argued that when compared to horses, camels could carry much heavier loads (in some cases 1,000-1,300 lbs.) And while horses and mules require hay or grass, camels flourish on prickly pear cactus and other desert plants. Finally, camels can go for days without water.

But cavalry horses would often stampede at the offensive odor peculiar to camels. Even Army teamsters, not known for excellent hygiene themselves, expressed loud displeasure at camel smells.

The U.S. Army's 1858 Survey of the Southwest employed camels during a campaign that sustained multiple attacks by hostile Indians. In one encounter, 14 soldiers mounted on camels successfully repelled an attack by 200 Indians.

Military camels lost their biggest "cheerleader" when James Buchanan became president, forcing Davis to relinquish his cabinet job. (Soon Jefferson Davis would gain a bigger job as president of the Confederacy.)

In time the Army grew weary of camels, and sought willing buyers. South Texas lawyer Bethel Coopwood bought 66 camels, and started a caravan business between Laredo and Mexico City. Unfortunately, raids by Mexican banditos exacted a heavy toll on his camel caravans.

Californian Sam McLaughlin also bought Army camels, and staged camel races for the amusement of crowds. When dromedary racing flopped, McLaughlin used his camels to haul tons of salt from remote mines. On one salt trek to Yuma, Ariz., McLaughlin suddenly died, whereupon his Arab drovers turned the entire camel herd loose in the Arizona desert. Thus began the 70-year odyssey of "wild" camels in America.

One rogue camel gained legendary status. It started in 1883, when a woman was trampled to death by an unknown beast that left behind reddish fur in a thorn bush. Later sightings and attacks confirmed the killer as a huge roan-colored camel. Arizona newspapermen christened it the "Red Ghost." Local Mexicans called the beast "Fantasia Colorado."

Arizonans were fascinated by the Red Ghost's vicious behavior, but even more fascinated by this bizarre fact: Strapped to its back was a dead rider!

Two prospectors later fired on the great camel, causing it to shake off the rider's mummified skull. The Red Ghost and its now headless rider continued to terrorize rural Arizona for years. In 1893 near Ore, Ariz., rancher Mizoo Hastings brought down the creature with one shot. The bones of its gruesome cargo had long since fallen away. But rawhide ropes were still embedded in the camel, with knots indicating the ropes could not have been tied by the rider. Someone had bound the mystery rider, dead or alive, to the Red Ghost's back.

The last reliable sighting of an American wild camel was near an Arizona waterhole in 1931. But a witness in Douglas, Texas, claimed to have seen a wild camel in 1941. Occasional reports of camel tracks in Arizona would persist through the 1950s.

The Red Ghost is gone. But diehards say wild camels, ghost or otherwise, might still wander the far corners of Arizona.

The Red Ghost

Dale Crawford

Hanging Judge Dispensed Swift Justice

"There is no Sunday west of St. Louis – and no God west of Fort Smith."
~ Old frontier adage

Just west of Fort Smith, Arkansas was Indian Territory, arguably the most godless, lawless and racist place in post-Civil War America. One insanely overworked federal courtroom maintained jurisdiction over western Arkansas and Indian Territory. Presiding was the famously efficient "Hanging Judge" Isaac Parker.

Read on to see why Parker later contended he was "…the most misunderstood man" in America.

Parker was an activist in the relatively new Republican Party, where he was selected for the Electoral College and cast his vote for Abraham Lincoln. Six years later he became a Missouri Congressman, championing Indian rights and espousing the then radical idea that women in U.S. territories should have the right to vote.

Years later, President Ulysses Grant sought a man to dispense federal justice in the 74,000-square-mile Indian Territory, a land with many Indian courts but no court with jurisdiction over non-Indian criminals. Parker was Grant's choice.

When Judge Parker arrived in Fort Smith, he promptly ordered the construction of a gallows big enough to hang 12 men at one time. In his first term of court, 18 people came before Parker on murder charges. Fifteen were convicted and sentenced to hang.

Hangings were public affairs in those days, with up to 5,000 spectators gathering in Fort Smith to witness multiple hangings. Newspapers avidly covered events for curious readers. Reporters dubbed Parker's courtroom the "Court of the Damned."

During the next two decades, Parker sentenced 160 men to death by hanging — half were actually hanged and the rest died in jail, were pardoned on appeal or killed in escape attempts. Parker reserved most of his sympathy for crime victims, becoming one of the first advocates of victim's rights.

Isaac Parker's frontier justice required an equally no-nonsense executioner. Enter George Maledon, a diminutive man who always dressed in black, rarely smiled and was generally shunned by Fort Smith citizens. Yet Maledon took a grim pride in his profession, and in the articles crowning him "Prince of Hangmen."

In retirement, Maledon displayed ropes, gallows beams and other relics in a traveling "tent show." From the podium he described how he hanged 88 men, being careful in each case to make the killing as humane as possible. "A big knot is necessary," said Maledon. "If it doesn't break the man's neck when he drops, he strangles. That isn't pretty. The knot must be put just behind the left ear so it will snap the neck when he drops."

Thanks to Parker's swift justice, Maledon ranks as the most prolific executioner in U.S. history.

Popular culture, then as now, demanded a one-dimensional "Hanging Judge." Yet in his sunset years, Parker lamented this simplistic image. He reminded the few who would listen that federal law at the time allowed just one punishment for murder or rape. He wrote, "In the uncertainty of punishment … lies the weakness of our halting justice."

Believe it or not, Isaac "Hanging Judge" Parker was opposed to the death penalty.

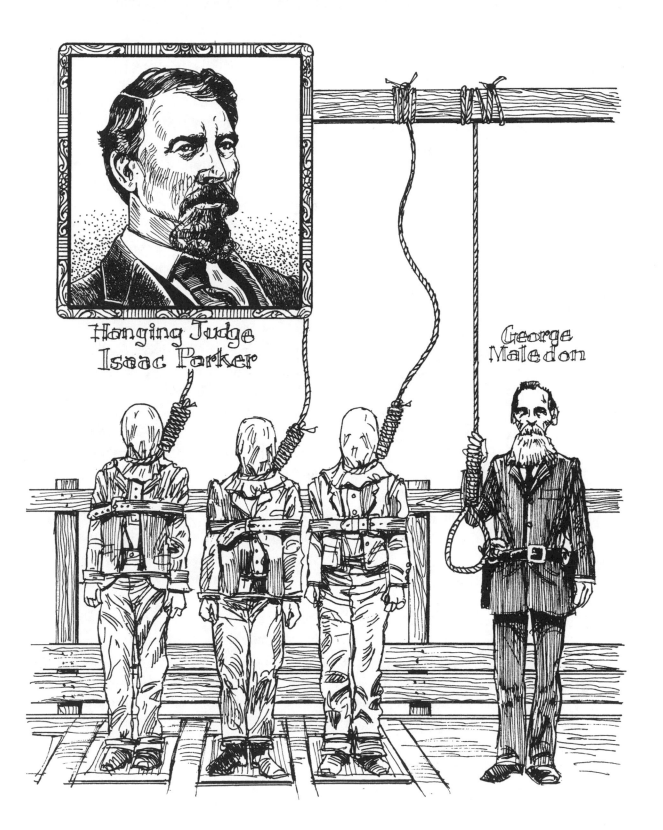

Hanging Judge
Isaac Parker

George
Maledon

Why Bread Always Falls Butter-side Down

For years, California has claimed Edwards Air Force Base as the birthplace of the phrase, "If anything can go wrong, it will," otherwise known as Murphy's Law. Folks in Wyoming beg to differ. You decide:

Many believe Murphy's Law was named in 1949 for Californian Capt. Edward Murphy, an engineer on a project to see how much sudden deceleration a human can withstand. Murphy helped design a rocket sled outfitted with a chair into which was strapped first a crash test dummy … then a chimpanzee … then finally a human, one Capt. John Stapp. Murphy wanted to more accurately measure the extreme g-forces Stapp experienced by using gauges attached to his harness.

Murphy instructed an assistant on installing the sensor gauges, and then ran a rocket sled test. When the gauges showed a "zero" gravity reading, it was discovered they were installed backwards — to which the disgruntled Murphy made his now-famous pronouncement. The project manager kept a list of "laws" and added this one, which he called Murphy's Law.

The phrase received public attention at a subsequent press conference, where Stapp was asked how it was that nobody had been severely injured during the rocket sled tests. Stapp's answer: They always took Murphy's Law into consideration. He explained the law, and how it motivated officers to consider all the possible things that could go wrong before conducting a test.

But there is this earlier claimant: In 1885, Wyoming Territory Justice of the Peace Billy Murphy learned the recently constructed Ames monument (see Mass. story page 58) sat on public land, not on railroad land as just about everyone else believed. Murphy promptly filed a $9.75 homestead claim, then informed dumbfounded Union Pacific Railroad officials that the monument was legally his. And he planned to sell advertising on it!

The great trackside monument was intended to honor the Ames brothers for leading the transcontinental railroad efforts. Having the monument covered in advertising was unacceptable to railroad officials, who promptly sent a armed delegation of three former lawmen and a lawyer, the latter carrying a mysterious black briefcase.

The delegation locked Murphy in a room, and then used falsehoods and intimidation followed by an offer to settle the matter by trading the monument land for a townsite lot valued at less than $400. Murphy saw no choice but to authorize the trade. Only later was it revealed that the lawyer's black briefcase contained $30,000 in cash and promissory notes, to be used as necessary.

For Billy Murphy, just about everything that could go wrong had gone wrong. The same could be said for the Union Pacific, as ironically the railbed was re-located, leaving the railroad's great monument standing in obsurity. This is evidence enough for Laramie attorney Jim Hand and others that Wyoming is indeed the birthplace of Murphy's Law.

California or Wyoming? You decide.

Murphy's Law

CALIFORNIA REPUBLIC

Captain Murphy

Rocket Sled

Highest Horse Captures Nation's Heart

Could a horse survive winter alone on the Colorado tundra at 13,000 feet? With a little help, yes…as proven in February, 1956. That's when a private pilot flying from Denver to Gunnison was stunned to see a big bay horse stranded on the barren, windswept saddle connecting 14,420 foot Mount Harvard and 14,196 foot Mount Yale. Mammoth snowfields blocked any descent to milder climes, and it seemed clear the horse would perish without food. Pilots from Gunnison volunteered to drop hay bales from small planes. Such dangerous flights amidst the icy gales of the Continental Divide prompted volunteer pilot Gordon Warren to say, "That horse was getting the kind of flying out of us that money could not buy."

The *Denver Post* was the first newspaper to see the story's potential. Other papers followed, both in America and around the world. *Post* reporters figured they needed a name for the unnamed horse. They chose Elijah, after the Biblical figure kept alive in the desert when God sent ravens to drop morsels of food.

Commercial airline pilots flying from Denver to Los Angeles altered their routes slightly to give passengers a glimpse of the famous "Horse in the Sky." An Air Force veteran offered to parachute onto the Continental Divide to keep Elijah company until snows melted. *LIFE* Magazine declared Elijah "… the most worried-about horse in the United States."

From aerial photos, Bill and Al Turner of Buena Vista became convinced that mysterious Elijah was actually their escaped trail horse named Bugs. They flew over the ridge to confirm it was indeed their horse. In April, the Turners led an unsuccessful attempt to rescue Elijah/Bugs. Near the end of May, they tried again. Though snows were still deep, the Turners and others shoveled their way to the horse, leading him down through narrow pathways in the snowfields.

Overnight, Coloradoans who awakened each morning to ask, "How's Elijah?" were now suddenly asking to actually see Elijah. Accordingly, a parade was organized through downtown Denver. Centennial Racetrack showcased Elijah in its winner circle, where officials draped the bewildered gelding with flowers and a colorful winner's blanket. A special stall was constructed in the lobby of the Brown Palace, and thus Elijah became one of the famed hotel's most unusual guests.

But Elijah was, after all, really just Bugs the mountain horse. And his handlers could see that this horse was increasingly unhappy in the big city. So festivities were cut short. Bugs was returned to his beloved alpine pastures, where he lived a long and uneventful life as a trail mount.

Bill Turner always maintained that this particular horse had an aversion to all things urban, especially automobiles and women in skirts — which is why, in the wintry weeks of the rescue attempts, a *Denver Post* columnist had raised a troubling possibility: "Perhaps this horse in the clouds does not wish to be rescued, but is exactly where he wants to be!"

Dale Crawford

Wacky Gold Rush Tales Abound

Just prior to the Civil War, Americans stampeded to Colorado in a gold rush followed by a rollicking silver rush. Many a covered wagon trekking westward carried this hand-painted message: "Pikes Peak or Bust."

Miners worked in often inhospitable locations — some as extreme as Moose Mine, which was situated just below 14,000 feet near the top of Mt. Bross. In 1886, three miners were covered by the snows of an avalanche northeast of Gunnison. Despite being encased in snow in ominously named Deadman Gulch, two of the three managed to dig themselves out. By this time a rescue party had arrived, and someone noticed a hand sticking out of the snow. They dug in, and found the third miner, still alive, and seated on his standing dead horse.

In that same decade, Leadville's Harrison Avenue was paved with shining "silver." The prevailing imperfect method of removing precious metals from ore left a fair amount of silver remaining in the smelter slag. This slag was used to pave Harrison Avenue. In Victor, a nearby highway was surfaced with similar leftover material from the rich Portland Mine. According to some mining experts, this highway would now assay at tens of thousands of dollars per mile.

Sometimes miners made mistakes, as when workers inadvertently started a fire in the Vulcan mine near Newcastle. The year was 1896, and that underground coal seam fire is still burning.

On the vast Uncompahgre Plateau, one mine yielded radium in the 1900s, vanadium in the 1920s and finally uranium in the 1950s, which was then the world's most sought-after mineral. In some cases, the same ore was put through the mill three times, paying off each time!

Miners in remote mining camps often had to come up with their own amusements. Horse racing and foot racing were popular, with considerable sums wagered on the outcome. To add incentive, a foot racer was occasionally allowed to run the race carrying the total dollars wagered on him. The winning runner would then receive a percentage of the winnings upon completion of the race.

In Grand Lake in 1883, the winner of one foot race had $4,000 hanging from his belt. When he dashed across the finish line, he just kept on sprinting right into the woods at the end of the street. Once in the woods, he jumped on a conveniently tethered race horse, and was never seen again!

Connecticut Yankee Is Forgotten First President

He was a great patriot and by some accounts was America's first president. He married a woman named Martha. When the first shots were fired in the American Revolution he was 43 — same age as the more famous George Washington. Who was this Samuel Huntington, and why is he erased from most popular histories?

Nearly any Connecticut history buff will proudly tell you of this forgotten native son. But first, you might have to listen to a few other big moments from this little state:

For example, there was a time when tiny Connecticut was really big. In early days, a colony's grant from the king extended from "sea to shining sea." Thus, colonial Connecticut claimed the northern portions of today's Pennsylvania, Ohio and beyond. Between 1769 and 1799, Connecticut and Pennsylvania contested these lands in the on-again, off-again conflict known as the Yankee-Pennamite War.

Connecticut eventually ceded northern Pennsylvania, but held stubbornly to northern Ohio, known then as the "Western Reserve." A half-million acres in the Reserve was awarded to Connecticut residents whose homes had been burned by the British. Called the Sufferer's Lands, these relocated settlements explain why the architecture and town plans of today's northern Ohio mimic New England.

In 1784, America's first law school opened in little Litchfield, Conn. For the next 100 years law schools were not only rare, but largely unnecessary. Many famous American lawyers never attended law school, among them Patrick Henry, Abe Lincoln, no fewer than four U. S. Supreme Court Chief Justices … and Samuel Huntington.

Huntington's family sent three of his brothers to Yale, but Samuel was self-educated in a rural neighbor's private law library. Never showy, Samuel nonetheless rose quickly by working hard and working smart. Before long he was appointed King's Attorney, then Connecticut's delegate to the Continental Congress, where he was one of the signers of the Declaration of Independence.

Huntington eventually became the presiding officer of the Continental Congress and was the first to be referred to as "President of these United States, in Congress Assembled."

Today's more powerful office of the presidency came later, with ratification of the U.S. Consitition. Thus, George Washington is rightly remembered as the first president of America's current political structure. But one is left to ponder if Washington modeled *his* presidential behavior — prudence, dignity, firm but quiet diplomacy — on that "other" first president, Connecticut's Samuel Huntington.

George Washington

S. Huntington

Feminine Touch Is "Kiss of Death"

Google "most wicked woman in America," and you'll find Delaware's Patty Cannon. Cannon and her gang kidnapped free blacks and sold them into slavery in the South. Their criminality was in effect a "reverse Underground Railroad."

Operating from her property straddling the Delaware-Maryland border, Cannon had advantages. With her house in one state and her barn in the other, Patty Cannon could conveniently evade lawmen from either state by simply walking across the barnyard. And Delaware, nominally a slave state, was in fact home to mostly free blacks — the logical targets of kidnappers.

Cannon's neighbors, like some other post-Colonial white Americans, viewed freemen suspiciously. Slaves, after all, posed no legal difficulty as they were simply property. Free blacks existed in a legal limbo. Neither slave nor full citizen, a free black person couldn't, for example, testify against a white person in court.

Typical of Cannon's many victims was the 25-year-old free black Lydia Smith, who was forcibly abducted and kept briefly in Cannon's home. Smith was soon moved to Cannon's son-in-law's tavern, where she was held in shackles in a hidden chamber for five months. She was then shipped south in a slave schooner and sold into bondage in Georgia.

The ironic seeds of this injustice are buried in Article 1, Section 9, of the U.S. Constitution, which expressly permits the brutal African slave trade — but only for 20 years. When that grace period expired in 1808, the price of slaves shot upward. This unintentionally increased the kidnapping of free blacks.

Patty Cannon's reign of terror finally ended in 1829, shortly after she rented land to a tenant farmer. When the farmer's plow uncovered human remains, authorities from Delaware and Maryland jointly arrested Cannon, charging her with four counts of murder. Victims included an infant female baby and two young male children — small inconveniencies that were disposable because they had no current value as slaves.

Before conviction, Cannon cheated the hangman by committing arsenic suicide in her Sussex County, Del., jail cell. With her burial in a nearby pauper's grave, Americans thought they had seen the last of Patty Cannon. Not quite.

As the years passed her legend grew, reaching mythic proportions in 1841 with the publication of the "Female Fiend" pamphlet. Her renown was stoked further by George Alfred Townsend's 1884 novel "The Entailed Hat," which was based on Cannon's life and times.

Things got weird in the 20th century when Sussex County decided to enlarge the courthouse, which required moving bodies from the pauper's graveyard. According to legend, when a young man helping with reburial learned he was working on Cannon's remains, he slipped Patty's skull into his jacket and took it home as a "gift" for his father, Alfred W. Joseph.

In 1963, Joseph walked into the Dover (Del.) Public Library with a hatbox and documents under one arm. "Would the library like an unusual addition to your collection of artifacts?" he asked. And with that he revealed the alleged skull of Patty Cannon. The papers were said to confirm her identity.

To this day, the library's archives contain the skull of that woman we want to forget, but can't …

Bug Bite Alters U.S. History

In its earliest days, America's seat of government dodged British soldiers by rotating the capital between Philadelphia, New York, Baltimore, Trenton and other communities. Later, in a concession to Southern states, the permanent capital was designated south of the Mason-Dixon Line in a special district straddling the Virginia-Maryland border. The actual site was handpicked by George Washington, who rather curiously chose a swampy flatland near his estate on the Potomac River. (Washington was the only U.S. president to never live in the federal capital named for him.)

The humid subtropical wetlands of the new capital were considered unhealthy. Some of the early presidents conducted business in the city, but then retreated to higher ground outside the District to sleep. Swamps meant mosquitoes, and mosquitoes meant malaria.

In fact, the United States may have gained Florida thanks to the bite of one mosquito. It happened in 1818, when President James Monroe was bedridden with what was probably malaria fever. A letter from General Andrew Jackson arrived at the White House, seeking presidential instruction regarding a possible invasion of Florida. After Jackson captured of Spanish Florida, Monroe claimed his permission was never granted. Jackson disagreed. This "massive misunderstanding" was likely due to Monroe's malaria delirium, leaving him unaware of the letter or its contents. The malaria-infested Potomac River was part of the morning ritual of athletic John Quincy Adams, our sixth president. Adams would typically rise early, walk to the Potomac,

disrobe, and swim. One morning his clothes were stolen. The skinny-dipping president then faced the undignified prospect of walking home naked. Instead, he persuaded a passing boy to run to the White House and fetch other clothes.

The roughshod new capital was home to just 14,000 persons when first occupied by federal government in November 1800. Of these souls, 3,244 were slaves.

It's common knowledge that many of the founding fathers were slave owners, but less known that 10 of the first 12 presidents owned slaves. Only the father-son presidental duo of John Adams and John Quincy Adams never owned slaves.

The last president to have owned a slave was, ironically, Ulysses Grant. This former top Union general in the Civil War served as chief executive until 1877. Grant freed one slave, William Jones, just two years before the Civil War flared. Grant also benefited from the many slaves his father-in-law gave his wife.

Thomas Jefferson owned 141 slaves. Andrew Jackson owned 160 slaves. At one time George Washington owned 216 slaves.

When he died in 1799, Washington's last will freed his manservant William Lee immediately, and stipulated a lifelong pension. The other slaves were to be freed when his widow died, according to the will. However, Martha chose to free them all two years later. Was it a gracious act? Not according to another First Lady: Abigail Adams always maintained that Martha's charity was because she feared her life might be in danger because her death meant freedom for the slaves.

James Monroe

John Q Adams

Ulysses Grant

Skull 'Speaks' of Prehistoric Kindness

A Stone Age people once returned again and again to a tiny pond in present-day suburban Titusville, Fla. The night sky was their calendar. The phases of the moon guided their every activity. Who among them could dream this nameless pond would be a great place to view rocket launches taking astronauts to that same moon?

The inconspicuous pond gained fame in 1982, when the development company EKS began excavations. After just a few scoops of earth, backhoe operators uncovered human bones. EKS halted construction, authorized radiocarbon dating, *and* generously spent $60,000 for pumps to enable the subsequent "wet" archaeological dig.

The results were stunning. What is now called Windover Pond contained the bodies of 168 individuals — some had died 7,000 years ago, others nearly 9,000 years ago. This ancient cemetery was hidden *under* the peat bog portion of the pond.

Archaeologists recovered more than 90 skulls. Many contained intact human brains! It seems the crania, so effective at protecting our brains when we're alive, is equally effective in death.

Like the less ancient remains of the celebrated "bog people" of Northern Europe, human tissue at Windover was preserved when peat and mineralized waters resulted in oxygen-free burials. No oxygen meant no bacteria and fungi, resulting in minimal decomposition.

The state of preservation suggests the deceased were buried quickly. Each was wrapped in a colored textile, the oldest known fabric discovered in the New World. The marvelously preserved brains provide the oldest group DNA samples ever discovered. Mysteriously, the Windover DNA shows no connection to modern Native Americans.

Another mystery is why these people would choose a pond for a cemetery. Some speculate that the soft bottom of the pond made for easy digging. Alternately, a spiritual people might have been attracted by the night glow of methane "swamp gas," as the rising methane bubbles appeared to "breathe" for those who had stopped breathing.

The remains at Windover are achingly human. In one burial a mother cradles her newborn. In another a 3-year-old was lovingly laid to rest holding her favorite toys.

But two skeletons from Windover proved especially enlightening. One was an elderly woman who had suffered multiple bone fractures years before.

The other skeleton was of a 15-year-old male victim of spina bifida, a crippling disease of the vertebrae. His left foot was severely deformed.

These two clan members clearly required a lot of attention and loving care — the woman through a lengthy convalescence and the boy for his entire life. In death they speak to us of an ancient society more caring and less nomadic than scientists had thought possible.

Natives Invent Alphabet, Build Nation

Decades before the Confederacy attempted to establish a separate nation within America, a smaller rebel nation-within-a-nation declared independence. It happened in 1820 in northern Georgia with the birth of the Cherokee Nation. The embattled Cherokee Indians saw nationhood as the only way to deal with encroachment from white settlers. Thus the Cherokee Nation created its own capital — New Echota, near present-day Calhoun, Ga. — a distinct Cherokee-language alphabet and national newspaper, a Supreme Court building, a written constitution, a national flag, a school system and an elected congress.

The Cherokee Nation even voted to fight alongside American troops in the Creek War, opposing Creek Indians who were supported by European powers.

The first chief of the Cherokee Nation was John Ross. Ross served beside Andrew Jackson in the Creek War, and by some accounts saved the future president's life in battle. Nevertheless, Jackson's claim to fame was as an Indian fighter, and he unsurprisingly demanded removal of the Cherokee and all other native peoples of the South.

For fifteen years the Cherokee used every peaceful means to retain their sacred homeland. By 1838 these efforts, including a seemingly successful appeal to the U.S. Supreme Court, were brushed aside as federal troops assembled the tribe at gunpoint for removal to Indian Territory in present-day Oklahoma.

Thus began the infamous Trail of Tears, a forced march of 1,000 miles in which upwards of one in five Cherokee perished.

Modern laws governing Indian tribes retain echoes of a time when tribes were considered nominally independent nations. This explains why casinos are allowed on reservations. In 1959, President Fidel Castro recognized the sovereignty of a Seminole Nation delegation arriving from Florida to Havana, Cuba. From 1969 to 1971, Indians occupied California's Alcatraz Island, established Radio Free Alcatraz, and attempted to negotiate as a sovereign state.

In February 1973, 200 Native American activists and some traditional Lakota elders occupied the village of Wounded Knee, SD (site of an 1890 massacre of Indians by the U.S. Army). They announced the creation of the Oglala Lakota Nation, and declared independence from the United States. The resulting armed siege lasted 71 days.

During World War I, young Native American males who were still not considered citizens eagerly volunteered to defend America. When these Indian warriors returned from the Great War, they ironically returned as foreigners to a homeland that was originally theirs. Congress recognized the absurdity, and granted immediate citizenship to any Native American who served in WWI. This left the emancipated soldier in the awkward position of having a wife and children unable to vote or enjoy other citizenship benefits.

By 1920 American women had at long last gained the right to vote...but not, of course, Native American women. Finally, in 1924 citizenship was granted to all Indians by an act of Congress. Perhaps not surprisingly, a few natives politely refused citizenship, preferring to remain members of their original tribal "nations."

John Ross

President
A. Jackson

Ꮭtlu
Ꮵtsu
Ꮹwu
Ꮿyu
iᴠ
Ꭱgv
Ꮽhv
Ꭷlv
Ꭴnv
Ꮛquv
Ꭱsv
Ꮝdv
Ꮲtlv Ꮳtsv Ꮼwv Ᏼyv

Sailors Shatter South Seas Tranquility

Life in ancient Hawaii was hardly "paradise." Hawaiians endured pagan rules known as taboos. One taboo prohibited females from consuming certain forbidden fruits. Another taboo required death by torture if one's dog barked during ritual silence.

Things changed in 1820 when missionaries reached Honolulu. The missionaries converted many islanders to Christianity, while introducing new taboos: hula dancing was prohibited, and the iconic Hawaiian shirt was invented to cover native nakedness.

In 1826 the first U.S. warship arrived when "Mad Jack" Percival piloted the *USS Dolphin* into Honolulu's harbor, and fired a cannon salute. Hearing no customary salute in reply, Percival took it as an insult to America. But he had fired his cannon on Sunday, and the now-devout Hawaiians simply waited until Monday to fire their cannon.

Percival was a legend among sea captains. He went to sea at age 13, and later commanded a U.S. Navy fleet pursuing Caribbean pirates. Percival is reputed to have navigated a ship from Africa to Brazil with his entire crew sick or dead of fever.

Yet even iron-fisted Percival struggled to maintain discipline among a *Dolphin* crew confined at sea for months. Percival promised that good behavior would earn his crew those legendary charms of Polynesian women. But no longer were Hawaiian girls allowed to swim out to the anchored ships. "Mad Jack" Percival was furious with this perceived affront to the American flag. Had not British sailors of the frigate *Blonde* recently enjoyed the customary "society" of Hawaiian females?

A face-to-face negotiation followed between the salty Percival and Queen Ka'ahumanu. She explained: recent translation of the Ten Commandments had impressed certain chiefs, who believed the verses made a fine code of laws for what was then called the Sandwich Islands.

Percival wouldn't be denied. On Sunday he issued the usual rum ration, and then pointedly allowed his men shore liberty. The angry sailors soon interrupted a native church service, breaking every window in the building.

The drunken mob then confronted lead missionary Hiram Bingham. A group of Hawaiian warriors, followers of Bingham, quietly looked on with war clubs in hand.

When one of the rioters struck Bingham, the Hawaiians clubbed the ringleaders senseless and drove the others back to their ship to swiftly end the "Battle of Honolulu." Soon Percival was back in the palace, where he admitted his men overreacted, but insisted the *Dolphin* wouldn't leave port until "recreational rights" were reinstated. Queen Ka'ahumanu concluded this man must be a pirate masquerading as a naval officer. Fearing more violence, she lifted the taboo.

Thanks to "Mad Jack," the custom of girls swimming to anchored ships returned to the islands as immortalized in this lusty sea shantie:

We're homeward bound!
'Tis a grand old sound on a good ship taut and free,
And we don't give a damn when we drink our rum with the girls on old Maui.
~ Rolling Down to Old Maui

Percival would later be cleared of misconduct by a naval court of enquiry. Yet many Americans were puzzled when in 1920 a new flagship destroyer was christened the *USS Percival*. Search "USS Percival Hawaii" for an ironic online image of this warship in Honolulu's harbor … presumably without the native women!

Mad Jack gets a message from the Queen

Mountain Mail Mania

What was the strangest item ever mailed through the U.S. Postal Service? Well, the mountain states of Idaho and Utah each have a compelling candidate.

When 4-year-old May Pierstorff begs and begs to visit grandma, there's a problem. Her parents can't afford to send her. In Idaho circa 1914, railroads are the only way to make the 75-mile trip over the mountains from Grangeville to Lewiston. A train ticket is too pricey, but the Pierstorffs come up with a novel solution: mailing May! You see, wee May weighs 48 1/2 lbs. — just under the Parcel Post limit of 50 lbs.

May rides all the way to Lewiston in the train's mail compartment with the required 53 cents in stamps pinned to her coat. Upon arrival, May is delivered to grandma's house by the train's mail clerk, who is conveniently her mother's cousin.

On the other extreme, Utah witnessed the largest item ever mailed: a bank building. It happened in 1916, when W. H. Coltharp began constructing the Bank of Vernal, Utah. He dreamed it would be the most modern building between Denver and Salt Lake City.

To accomplish his goal, Coltharp would need special textured bricks. But the nearest source of these hard-fired bricks was Salt Lake City, many treacherous miles away via narrow-gauge railroad and horse-drawn freight wagon.

The freight charge alone would be four times the value of the bricks. Coltharp's solution? Bundle the bricks 10-to-a-box, and send 'em via Parcel Post.

Soon postal workers across Utah were frantic as tons of bricks began to pile up. The Postmaster General and other leaders in Washington noted the chaos. This led to federal mail regulations limiting any single postal customer to no more than 200 lbs. mailed daily, but not before Coltharp received all 80,000 of his precious bricks. Locals jokingly called it the "Parcel Post Bank," and you can still see this building at 3 Main St., Vernal, Utah.

There's another curious Rocky Mountain mail story about the mailman who didn't "go postal," but rather just the opposite. Civil War tensions were high in Colorado Territory, circa 1863, when a crowd in Canon City seized a man named Burr, accusing him of belonging to a gang of Confederate sympathizers. Burr was to be hanged on the spot, the rope already around his neck, when the town's mailman persuaded the crowd to spare the man's life. When asked why he intervened, the mailman's explanation was simple: He had a letter for Burr!

Dale Crawford

Aviator is World's Luckiest Man

"The Luckiest Man Alive." This was the moniker given Chicago's John Hedley by a foreign war correspondent in 1918. We now know this wasn't newspaper hype:

Born in Northumberland, England in 1887, this future American led a mostly uneventful life until the beginning of the First World War. That's when Hedley joined the Royal Air Corps. As an aviator, he gained "ace" status by shooting down 11 German aircraft.

Hedley's short stature made him the perfect "tail gunner" for a Bristol F2B biplane, the primitive British war plane that author Alan Axelrod called a "coffin with wings."

By 1917, the average life expectancy of a British aviator serving on the Western Front was three weeks! Captain Hedley was beating those odds until a fateful day in January 1918 when the unthinkable happened:

Hedley and pilot Reginald Makepeace were three miles above the French countryside in a dogfight with German fighter planes. When Makepeace suddenly put the plane into a nosedive to evade attack, Hedley abruptly fell out of his seat into the open air. Makepeace knew his comrade was lost, and continued the rapid descent for several hundred feet.

When the plane pulled up, a free-falling Hedley was able to grab the tail and clamor back into his seat! The plane's steep descent apparently created a downdraft that took Captain Hedley with it at a speed equal to the aircraft.

Badly shaken, Hedley and Makepeace returned safely to base. Of course Hedley's brush with death didn't excuse him from further aerial combat. Later that year Hedley and K.R. Kirkham were flying a Bristol in a dogfight with the legendary Red Baron and his Flying Circus of fighter planes. Sources conflict, but some say Baron von Richthofen's bright red plane was the one that shot down Hedley and Kirkham.

Hedley's "flying coffin" crashed behind German lines, and his luck held again when both men walked away uninjured. Some would call this another miracle, for during those years the Germans issued parachutes to their aviators — but not the British. The Brits believed that parachutes would diminish the aggressive spirit of their pilots and tail gunners.

Hedley languished in a German prisoner-of-war camp until after the war. Upon his release, Hedley came to America, gained U.S. citizenship, and began a highly successful national speaking tour. Inside lecture halls in places like Joliet and Elgin Illinois, John Hedley regaled overflow crowds, while outside the marquee said it all: The Luckiest Man Alive.

After peddling his fame in the Roaring Twenties, John Herman Hedley retreated to a very private life in Chicago. But he had one final chapter to "write" in his book of luck. Hedley would live to see his 90th birthday in 1977. A male born in 1887 had a life expectancy of 41 years.

Honor Before Fame in Capone's Chicago

Chicago's past is rich with intriguing characters, such as Prohibition-era mobster Al Capone. And don't forget Capone's lawyer, "Easy Eddie." After all, it was Eddie's astute legal maneuvering that kept Big Al out of jail. In return, Capone rewarded Easy Eddie handsomely.

Life as an accomplice of Al Capone meant nice clothes, big houses, fast cars, and notoriety. Everybody knew Eddie, and he enjoyed living like a mobster. But if Eddie had one soft spot, it was his son. And while he could shower his only son with material possessions, Eddie felt powerless to pass on the integrity of a good name.

Ultimately, Eddie was determined to clean up his tarnished family name by testifying against the mobsters. He knew the cost could be great, but this was his gift to his son. Eddie's testimony resulted in a conviction and jail time for Al Capone. One week before Capone's release from Alcatraz, Easy Eddie was gunned down in a hail of bullets at a lonely Chicago intersection.

Those same Chicago streets spawned a hero of the Second World War: Lt. Commander. E. H. Butch O'Hare. He was a fighter pilot assigned to the carrier Lexington. One day Butch was forced to return from a mission because of low fuel. That's when his plane was unexpectedly the only defense between the American fleet and a fast-approaching squadron of Japanese fighter-bombers.

Laying aside personal safety, Butch dove into the surprised enemy formation, scattering those he didn't succeed in shooting down. Thus, Butch became the first Navy "ace" of the war and the first naval aviator to win the Congressional Medal of Honor.

Butch O'Hare climbed into his cockpit many more times, and ultimately died in aerial combat. But Chicago never forgot this native son. Think of him the next time you fly through O'Hare International Airport, for it is his namesake.

And there's one more thing: Butch's selfless integrity in wartime came at least partly from the reformed character of his late father, Easy Eddie O'Hare.

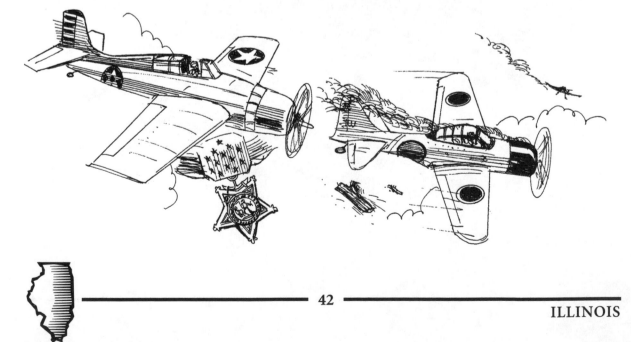

Grand Dragon's Fall Derails Klan

Ironically, the Ku Klux Klan reached its zenith of political power not in some southern commonwealth, but in "northern" states like Indiana and Colorado. The year was 1924, and in the Hoosier State the KKK infiltrated both major parties. In fact, the Republican Party nominated and elected a Klan governor and Klan majorities in both houses of the legislature. In those days the most powerful man in Indiana wasn't Governor Ed Jackson, but the man responsible for his election: D.C. Stephenson, state Grand Dragon of the KKK.

Stephenson was part of a nationwide resurrection of the post-Civil War Klan following the 1915 release of "The Birth of a Nation," America's first blockbuster feature film. The movie was based on the book *The Clansman* by Thomas Dixon, and scene after scene romanticized the role of the KKK as patriotic defenders of American values. When Dixon, a former classmate to President Woodrow Wilson, arranged a White House screening, Americans flocked to the new epic.

Millions donned white robes to proclaim an Aryan vision of America. Klavens sprung up in every state. In Indiana, African-Americans were targeted, but also Jews, socialists, immigrants and Catholics. Klan members circulated rumors of a Vatican conspiracy to take over the world. In later years believers in this myth routinely tore the so-called papal mark, which resembles the pope's mitre hat, off the corner of dollar bills.

Nationwide, an estimated one in eight eligible male Americans took the membership oath. By 1924, Indiana Klan organizers had recruited nearly one-third of the state's white, Protestant males. This was Indiana's unbeatable voting block, all controlled by D.C. Stephenson.

But the Klan's reign in Indiana would be spectacularly short, for within months Grand Dragon Stephenson was convicted in a murder trial that gripped the nation. Publicly a strict Prohibitionist and defender of "Protestant womanhood," Stephenson was sentenced to life in prison for the abduction, forced intoxication, sadistic rape and eventual death of Madge Oberholtzer. During the rape, Stephenson had fiercely bitten the young woman so many times that one man described her as having been "chewed by a cannibal."

When the anticipated pardon from Governor Jackson didn't arrive, a vengeful Stephenson released long lists of public officials in many states who were on the Klan's payroll. This was the beginning of the end of the KKK as a political force … in Indiana and across America.

But during the KKK's "golden era," tens of thousands of Klansmen in hooded regalia paraded down Washington's Pennsylvania Avenue in a show of strength reportedly witnessed by President Calvin Coolidge. Peek at this list of famous card-carrying members of the KKK: President Warren G. Harding, future President Harry S. Truman, Mount Rushmore and Stone Mountain sculptor Gutzon Borglum, future Supreme Court Justice Hugo Black, at least eight U.S. senators, four governors and countless other public figures.

11148

D. C. Stephenson

KKK

Gritty Girl Saves the Day

The year was 1912. A black-curtained train pulled slowly out of Moingona Station with one purpose — to convey its sad cargo to the Boone, Iowa, cemetery. No, this wasn't the funeral cortège for some American president, but a special train courtesy of the North-Western Railroad to honor the stunning heroism of a former employee.

This is the story of Kate Shelley, born to peasants in Ireland but raised in fertile Iowa on a homestead by the railroad tracks near Moingona. To supplement a farm income, Kate's father took a railroad job. When he was killed in service to North-Western, the farming and hunting chores fell to 12-year-old Kate. Kate's bed-ridden mother and younger siblings could offer scant help.

Three years later, the storm of the century struck central Iowa. Kate peered from her window as a locomotive's light approached the nearby Honey Creek Bridge. When suddenly the headlight was gone, Kate knew the bridge had washed away, plunging the train into the ravine.

Not hesitating, Kate grabbed her father's old railroad lantern and dashed into the storm. From the high trestle, she heard faint cries above the thunder. Kate shouted back that she would summon help.

Even as she reassured the two survivors, Kate knew the Midnight Express with 200 passengers would soon round the curve and plunge over the same washed-out bridge — a disaster only she could avert by alerting the staff at Moingona Station.

In her life's defining moment, Kate resolved to reach the station in the only possible way, via the 600-foot-long, 170-foot-high trestle over the churning Des Moines River. The train bridge wasn't designed for foot traffic, forcing Kate to jump from one cross-tie to the next. Halfway across, the lantern failed. Kate dropped to her hands and knees, her only illumination the flashes of lightning.

Upon reaching the other side, Kate was bloody and exhausted. But there was no stopping now. She sprinted the remaining half mile to Moingona, burst into the depot, sounded the alarm and fainted. Having saved the express train, a revived Kate led a rescue train back to the bridge where the survivors were hanging on for dear life.

Soon this skinny girl was a national heroine. The Iowa legislature awarded her half a load of coal and a gold medal. The North-Western Railroad provided cash awards, a pass for life, and later offered high-paying jobs. Kate declined every job offer, as each required leaving her invalid mother. Later when the stationmaster position opened at nearby Moingona, Kate happily accepted the job.

Yet life remained as it always had been for spinster Kate. To stand in her humble farmyard one wouldn't guess it was home to a national heroine — unless you noticed each passing train respectfully tooting and slowing, or even stopping, on the nearby tracks.

Years later the old Des Moines River trestle was replaced by the world's longest double-track railroad span. It was christened Kate Shelley High Bridge, America's first bridge named for a woman.

Following Kate's death from appendicitis, some have claimed her strong spirit still roams near Moingona Station. Should you ever find yourself hiking that railroad right-of-way during a storm, poet MacKinley Kantor offers this advice:

"Be sure to take a lantern flame
To keep your spirit warm
For there will be a phantom train,
And foggy whistle cries –
And in the lightning flare you'll see
Kate Shelley on the ties."

Rip-Roaring Town is Cowboy Capital

What was the wildest and woolliest of all the Wild West towns? Maybe it was Deadwood, or Dodge City, or Tombstone. But many would vote for Trail City in far western Kansas. Today you can park your car on the shoulder of Highway 50 on the Kansas-Colorado border and walk south to the site of Trail City. There you will hear nothing but wind, and see nothing — except for the crumbling foundation of a hotel. But in its heydays of 1885-1886, Trail City bristled with activity. Here is the story of the rapid rise and fall of Trail City:

Shortly after the Civil War, Texans returning from military service discovered they could make a tidy profit by gathering the semi-wild Longhorn cattle on their ranches, and trailing them to Kansas railroad towns like Abilene and Dodge City — there to be shipped to Eastern markets. Sometimes the cattle were trailed further north to be fattened on lush Montana grasses.

But by the middle 1880s, the Great Plains was growing more settled and fenced, making large cattle drives increasingly impractical. To forestall the end of their industry, Texas cattlemen and contract drovers petitioned Congress to create a "National Cattle Trail" further to the west. This trail, a portion of which ran along the Colorado-Kansas border, was never formally approved by Congress. But it was in de facto use for years.

Because of this proposed federal road for cattle, a new trail town was needed at a point where the trail crossed the Arkansas River and the Santa Fe Railroad. Some envisioned it as a sort of "Cowboy Capital." Thus was born rip-roaring Trail City in the summer of 1885.

Several factors combined to make Trail City especially notorious. Being a major stopover on the trail, this was a place were cowboys were paid in cash. The town was decidedly "wide open," with the nearest court of law a full 75 miles away in Las Animas, Colo. Prostitutes were readily available. As special entertainment for visiting cowhands, the soiled doves of Trail City are reputed to have occasionally disrobed and mounted horses, to gallop naked from one end of Main Street to the other.

Saloons lined the east side of the street (author Al Look claimed there were 27). Each had a front door facing Colorado, but a back door that opened to Kansas! Thus, a fugitive from Colorado lawmen could simply exit the back door to Kansas, and freedom. Or vice versa. Other barroom shenanigans revolved around the fact that in those days Kansas was a "dry" state that banned alcohol. Thus, the empty booze bottles were often mockingly thrown out windows on the Kansas side.

Trail City earned its nickname "Hellhole on the Arkansas." But infamy was short-lived. A population of 500 in 1886 dwindled to a mere 50 by 1887, and Trail City faded away with the last of the great cattle drives.

Epic Quake Reroutes Mighty Mississippi

You might be anticipating America's biggest earthquake on the West Coast. But seismologists say the "Big One" already happened … in the Midwest!

Three titanic quakes in the winter of 1811-1812 wrought devastation over five future states, hitting western Kentucky especially hard.

A rare eyewitness account is found in the diary of frontiersman George Crist, who lived 150 miles from the epicenter near present-day Owensboro, Ky. His desperate entries record the quakes, and many of the 2,000 aftershocks:

"There was a great shaking of the earth this morning … The roar I thought would leave us deaf if we lived."

"If we do not get away from here the ground is going to eat us alive. Many people believe this is the beginning of the end of time."

Indeed, it looked like the end of time. Directly above the epicenter, the mighty Mississippi River stopped, then for a time flowed backward! Temporary waterfalls formed, islands disappeared, and for 140 miles the river's course was altered. Large new lakes appeared, while other lakes dried up. Geysers of sand and water spewed sulfur vapors (sulfur is the Biblical "brimstone"). Skyward, the unrelated yet foreboding Great Comet of 1811 appeared before and during the quakes.

The second quake came five weeks after the first. Eliza Bryan's diary contained this Jan. 23 entry: "… from this date until the 4th of February the earth was in continual agitation, visibly waving as a gentle sea."

The great quakes shook the continent — teacups rattled in Philadelphia, clocks stopped in Boston, church bells rang unaided in Virginia. We'll never know how big it was, as the Richter scale hadn't been invented. But years later Charles Richter estimated the New Madrid episode – named for New Madrid, Mo. – at 8.0 or greater.

The April 18 *St. Louis Gazette* noted "… a general peace among the Indians, and it is said the earthquakes created this pacification."

Scientists puzzle over how the New Madrid quakes formed so far from typical "hot" zones where tectonic plates meet, such as the San Andreas Fault. The New Madrid area still averages three tremors a week. Although most are never felt, one to two annual quakes are large enough to be noticed. Some experts predict a repeat of New Madrid, which would devastate levees, bridges and brick structures from Memphis to St. Louis, and impact 11 million Americans.

In this curious legacy of the historic quakes, a rerouted Mississippi River loped off the extreme western tip of Kentucky, "moving" it to the opposite side of the river. Reachable only via Tennessee, this 18-square-mile enclave is separated from the balance of the Bluegrass State by the river *and* a chunk of Missouri real estate. Kentuckians claim theirs is the only state with such a noncontiguous piece of land. Turn to page 110 to see why other states beg to differ.

Missouri

New Madrid

Mississippi River

Kentucky

Tennessee

Mother of All Logjams Blocks Waterway

Louisiana's Red River was the site of history's most famous logjam. It all started in the Dark Ages, when a few floating trees tangled above present-day Natchitoches, La., then built steadily over the centuries as floodwaters swept trees from riverbanks as far away as New Mexico. One by one, dead trees became part of what was known as the "Great Raft."

Witnesses reported the Great Raft extended upstream for at least 180 miles and perhaps as many as 250 miles, with only occasional gaps of visible open water. The logs jammed so tightly that soil accumulated on top of the raft, supporting vegetation that included small living trees. One might walk cross the raft and not realize there was a river below.

By some accounts the log jam started as early as 1200 AD. It's certain the Great Raft was well established by 1542, when historian Frank Schambach believes the gold-seeking Spanish conquistadors of explorer Hernando de Soto encountered the Raft on their return march to the Gulf of Mexico. The Spaniards would have preferred to follow the Red River southward, but this proved impossible due to vast "raft lakes" caused by the blockage of the main channel. Shortly thereafter, French explorers marked the Great Raft on maps as "Embarras d'Arbres," meaning "the blockage of trees."

When the Red River valley was settled, steamboats were the chief mode of transporting freight, explaining why residents of Louisiana and Arkansas petitioned Congress to remove the Great Raft. Their cause was strengthened by the fact that the Red River formed the international border between America's Louisiana Purchase and New Spain, prompting a call for forts and gunboats along the river.

Finally, in 1832, Secretary of War Lewis Cass ordered riverboat captain Henry Miller Shreve to use his new invention to clear the Great Raft. So powerful was Henry's design, a snagboat dubbed the *Heliopolis*, that he could clear the worst logjams. When he ultimately cleared the Great Raft, Shreve became a hero to the people of northern Louisiana. In gratitude they named a new steamboat landing in his honor: Shreveport, Louisiana was open for steamboat business, thanks to Capt. Henry Shreve!

There were two surprising consequences of the logjam removal: When the Red River began flowing rapidly, it cut a new channel at Natchitoches, which overnight went from being head of navigation to being a woeful four miles west of the great river. Shreveport, on the other hand, benefited from an unintended return of the logjam just upstream, making it the new head of navigation and one of the world's great shipping ports for cotton. It also ensured that Shreveport would become Louisiana's capital during the Civil War.

And while Capt. Shreve may have been a hero, he was no saint. Back in 1835 Shreve Town Company was formed by businessmen at the site of Capt. Shreve's camp. When a rival group started a nearby town called Coates Bluff, Shreve Town Company hired Capt. Shreve to divert the river slightly. He did so, leaving Coates Bluff without access to the Red River and assuring the ascendancy of Shreveport.

Despite man's best efforts, the Great Raft reformed every few years, although by 1882 the river was permanently opened with explosives and steam saws. But it was too late — by then rails, not rivers, were the avenues of commerce.

De Soto's conquestadors
encounter The Raft

The Snagboat
HELIOPOLIS

Birdbrain Treaty Puts Isle in Limbo

In grade school we learned that Canada and America are utterly peaceful neighbors that share the longest undefended border in the world. However, no one ever told us of a tiny island that is a pimple on otherwise smooth relations between the nations: Machias Seal Island — is it Maine, or is it Canada?

This treeless island in the Bay of Fundy covers barely 16 acres. It's that speck of U.S. soil where the morning sun first strikes — if indeed it *is* U.S. soil.

Boundary disputes involving Maine started early. Britian coveted Maine's towering white pines because of a shortage of tall timber in England appropriate for ship masts. A 1691 English law required Maine pines 24 inches or more in diameter and within three miles of water to be marked with an arrow, reserving them for the Royal Navy.

A dozen years after Maine seceded from Massachusetts to become a state, British Canada built and occupied a lighthouse on Machias Seal Island, and claimed prime logging country on the disputed mainland woods. By 1839, Maine was desperate to establish sovereignty, and became the first and only state to individually declare war on a foreign power.

As Maine congressman F.O.J. Smith of Maine explained, "The primary responsibility of federal government is to defend its own territory and citizens, but if the Government chooses to not live up to its obligations, Maine will defend its territory alone." Only after Maine sent volunteers to battle English troops did a reluctant Congress authorize 50,000 federal troops to join the so-called Aroostook War. All-out war was averted and the border issue settled — well, *almost* settled — by the Treaty of London.

Vague language in the treaty failed to assign ownership of Machias Seal Island. To this day the United States bases its sovereignty on the 1783 Treaty of Paris, which ended the American Revolution. Canada claims ownership based on having manned a lighthouse on the island since 1832. (It's probably no coincidence that every lighthouse on the East Coast of Canada is automated *except* for the staffed Machias Seal Island lighthouse.)

Why would either country care? The island has no strategic value, and no known minerals. The *raison d'etre* may be the adjacent lobster fishery. Prior to the 20th century, Maine residents considered lobsters disgusting scavengers and thus fit only as a survival food, or more likely as fertilizer. But tastes have changed. The island also has the best seabird watching in North America, including a large colony of lovable Atlantic Puffins.

Bird-watching tour boats from both nations converge on the island daily. Canadian tour captain Peter Wilcox grows weary of the ownership dispute. "People ask whose it is, and I say, 'whose flag is flying?' and leave it at that. It's a dead issue that will never be resolved." Maine tour captain Barna Norton claimed family ownership, stubbornly carrying a U.S. flag on every visit. Norton's lifelong dream of seeing Old Glory permanently snapping in the breeze above the island ended with his 2004 death at age 89.

Both countries *do* agree to limit visitors to protect the breeding birds. And so it is that one dozen Canadians may visit Machias Seal Island each morning and one dozen Americans each afternoon.

Maine

Canada

Grand Manan Channel

Machias Seal Island

How Maryland Fooled the British

With its capital rotating between 10 cities, what America really needed in 1790 was a permanent seat of government. What it got was the District of Columbia. The location, straddling the Maryland-Virginia border, was a "thank you" to Southern states for their more prompt repayment of Revolutionary War debt. When Virginia later took back its land contribution to the federal district, Maryland became the District's only real estate donator.

This capital would be invaded but once, by British soldiers during the War of 1812. The British occupied Washington for just 26 hours — time enough for disciplined soldiers to torch many public buildings even as they spared private residences. As the invaders moved down Pennsylvania Ave. and closer to the White House, President James Madison departed on horseback. According to legend, he carried with him the entire U.S. treasury in a strongbox.

First Lady Dolley Madison stayed in the White House after the president left. She stayed after her bodyguards left. She stayed to secure state papers and oil paintings. She stayed until she could hear the shouts of the advancing invaders.

The British then sacked and burned the unoccupied White House. Fires that night were visible from Baltimore. By morning a hurricane arrived to douse the smoldering flames, saving portions of the White House and other buildings.

Britain's mighty navy then sailed up Chesapeake Bay, lobbing cannonades at targets like Baltimore's Fort McHenry. These were the "bombs bursting in air" that inspired our national anthem.

After the British successfully invaded Washington, D.C., they were oddly thwarted in a like plan to capture the tiny shipbuilding hamlet of St. Michaels, Maryland.

The Miracle of St. Michaels began when a British deserter said the village was to be bombarded and invaded on the night of Aug. 10, 1814. Defenses were hastily organized, but proved meager: a volunteer militia armed with muskets, and one six-pound cannon.

That's when American General Perry Benson ordered lanterns to be placed in tree-tops just outside of town, relying on nimble children to carry the beacons to the highest branches. Other lanterns were hung from the topmasts of anchored tall ships. Then every other light in town was extinguished, creating history's first military blackout.

Night fell. The deception worked. British marines aimed their cannon fire at the lights, overshooting the town. However, a single errant cannonball crashed through the roof of the Merchant home, rolled across the attic floor and bounced lazily down the staircase, chasing an alarmed Mrs. Merchant and infant to the main floor.

Dawn revealed that only the Merchant house had been hit. That dwelling, to this day a private residence, is celebrated as "The Cannonball House." The clever defense earned St. Michaels its nickname: "The Town That Fooled the British."

Fame Is Fleeting for Pyramid Builders

There was a Massachusetts family so powerful that one might mention them in the same breath as the Kennedys — that is if they weren't all but forgotten. So influential were the Ames brothers that a great pyramid was erected in their honor on a wind-swept Wyoming mountain pass.

In 1803, the powerfully built blacksmith Oliver Ames moved his shovel-making company to Easton, a village south of Boston. Sons Oliver Jr. and Oakes soon joined the business. Their timing was perfect — picks and shovels were in high demand in frontier America. In the Mississippi Valley, sturdy Ames shovels were considered legal tender — accepted in lieu of cash. Even now, you may have an Ames tool hanging in your garage.

During the Civil War, Oakes Ames was elected to Congress. Abraham Lincoln became convinced that a transcontinental railroad was critical to holding the fragile Union together. But with track-laying progress painfully slow, Lincoln summoned Congressman Ames to the White House. Historians believe Lincoln's words went something like this: "Ames, you take hold of this. By building this [railroad] you will be the remembered man of your generation." Oakes seized the opportunity, as did brother Oliver, who in 1866 ascended to the presidency of the Union Pacific Railroad. Together they organized Credit Mobilier, the Union Pacific's financial arm.

With big brother Oakes twisting arms in Congress, and little brother Oliver calling the shots at the Union Pacific, their dream of a transcontinental railroad gained steam. On May 10, 1869, Americans celebrated what was then equivalent to landing a man on the moon — the driving of the "Golden Spike" signaling the line's completion. Back in Boston, the Oakes brothers basked in their glory. It appeared Abe Lincoln had been right — Oakes Ames might indeed be "…the remembered man of his generation."

But the Ames brothers' world soon collapsed. In 1872, the *New York Sun* exposed America's first great financial scandal. Of $47 million in government subsidies granted to Credit Mobilier, the Union Pacific booked $21 million as profit while contractors and workers went unpaid.

Many congressmen had bought Credit Mobilier stock and then voted favors for the railroad. But Oakes took the brunt of the heat. He was censured by Congress, and returned to Massachusetts in disgrace where he died two months later. Oliver was dead within four years. Most of Credit Mobilier's prominent promoters escaped trouble, including congressman and future president James Garfield.

The board of the Union Pacific felt the Ames brothers deserved better. They voted to immortalize the brothers with a 60-foot stone pyramid on the highest point of the transcontinental railroad, an obscure siding west of Cheyenne, Wyo., at 8,240 feet — then the highest rails in the world. The pyramid was topped by base-relief stone portraits of the Massachusetts siblings.

For a few years the monument was visible to all passing trains, prominent on a knoll adjacent to the tracks. But fame is fickle. At the turn of the century the railroad was re-routed three miles to the south. Also bypassed by Interstate 80, today the great pyramid stands utterly alone on a treeless plateau, accessible only by a winding dirt road.

Check out the California tale on page 20 for more curious facts about this monument.

Oaks

Oliver

Dale Crawford

Custer's Hobby Proves Deadly

If George Armstrong Custer hadn't been slain by Sioux warriors at the Battle of the Little Bighorn, there's evidence that his favorite hobby would have killed him!

Though born just across the border in Ohio, Custer's boyhood home was in Monroe, Mich. Monroe was also the hometown of his wife, Elizabeth.

Custer gained well-deserved fame as the Civil War "Boy General" (he was only 23 when promoted to brevet brigadier general) by gallantly leading units of Michigan cavalry or Michigan infantry.

Flambouyant and perhaps the best self-promoter of his era, Custer did and still does attract admirers and critics in equal numbers. Custer was so well regarded at the close of the Civil War that he was asked to be present when Robert E. Lee surrendered at Appomattox. Afterward Custer was given the very table on which the surrender papers were signed.

Yet this is the same man who finished last in his class at West Point. He was court-martialed not once, but twice — the second time for desertion when he walked away from his command for an extended visit with his wife. Inexplicably, Custer also ordered the summary execution of some of his enlisted men found guilty of desertion.

Custer's favorite hobby was hunting, one of two hobbies to nearly kill him. Once while pursuing a bull buffalo on horseback, the prey turned predator. In Custer's panicked effort to shoot the charging beast, he shot his own horse out from under himself. Somehow he managed to evade the buffalo on foot and limped back to camp with neither horse nor meat.

The other hobby? Custer was a partially self-taught but very accomplished taxidermist. He was introduced to the hobby by another taxidermist on a Great Plains military expedition in 1873. George took to taxidermy the way he took to everything in life: with gusto.

In those days large volumes of arsenic were required to prepare mounted specimens. Taxidermists were just beginning to understand why so many in their vocation were dying as young men.

By the time of the Little Bighorn battle, portions of Custer's blonde locks were falling out, and he was suffering from other signs of arsenic poisoning. Matthew Switlik, former director of the Monroe County, Mich. Historical Museum, suggests that if Custer hadn't died in the famous battle he probably would have died soon after from arsenic poisoning!

Incidentally, the Battle of the Little Big Horn occurred a few days before the planned celebration of American's Centennial on July 4, 1876. News of the Indian victory and the complete destruction of Custer's command traveled slowly in those days, reaching large Eastern cities just in time to dampen the Centennial celebrations.

The Little Big Horn wasn't just tough on George, but quite literally decimated the Custer men folk. On that day the family lost five men: Colonel Custer, brothers Thomas Custer and Boston Custer, a brother-in-law and a nephew.

Tower Foreshadows Rise and Fall of Foshay

Wilbur Foshay's life was changed forever by a youthful trip to Washington, D.C. The teenager was awestruck by America's then-tallest structure, the Washington Monument. This isn't surprising, for Foshay was really a Fouchée, a direct descendant of Joseph Fouchée, who was a key player in the French Revolution and an ardent admirer of George Washington's American Revolution. Young Wilbur dreamed of being successful enough to one day memorialize his hero George Washington.

In 1917, the art student-turned-business-man brokered a $6,000 investment in America's fledging utilities industry into a $22-million fortune. Needing a corporate headquarters in hometown Minneapolis, Foshay proposed a 32-story, 450-foot-tall building — the first skyscraper west of the Mississippi (Indeed, the building is only blocks west of that great river.)

Foshay Tower ruled the skies of Minneapolis until 1974, when the IDS Center topped 792 feet. Many other new buildings also dwarfed the venerable Foshay.

IDS Center was tall *and* architecturally innovative. Its unique stepback design transforms a rectangular unit that would typically have just four corner offices per floor into a building with 32 corner offices per floor!

The IDS Center may be Minnesota's tallest building, but nothing could top the colorful three-day grand opening of the Foshay Tower in 1929. It was the most extravagant party in the state's history. Foshay spared no expense — thousands of invited guests, including cabinet members, senators and congressmen, each received a commemorative gold watch. They were treated to banquets, and entertained by half-nude dancers. There were tours of Foshay's private office and home on the top floors — a gilded suite lined with African mahogany and bathrooms sporting gold-plated faucets.

Foshay commissioned John Philip Sousa to compose and perform a march for the occasion. Thus, Sousa and his 80-member band played, for the one and only time, "The Foshay Tower-Washington Memorial March." Afterward Foshay presented Sousa a check for $20,000.

But financial storm clouds were gathering. Only weeks after the grand opening, "Black Monday" ushered in the Great Depression. Foshay's empire unraveled. He lost ownership of the Tower before he even moved in. Embarrassingly, the check to John Philip Sousa bounced. Outraged, Sousa forbade performances of Foshey's march. In band circles, the composition became known as Sousa's "mystery march." (In 1988, a group repaid Foshay's debt to Sousa's estate, thus resurrecting the former "mystery march." Today you can listen for 99 cents per download.)

Things got worse. Foshay was convicted for investment fraud. Though later pardoned and exonerated by presidents Roosevelt and Truman, Foshay spent years in Leavenworth Penitentiary.

From his cell, Wilbur was consoled by having fulfilled his dream of youth — His tower, nick-named "Minnesota's Washington Monument", was a tapered obelisk inspired by the original. The first architectual design to receive a U.S. patent, the structure is like no other building in the world. Among concrete skyscrapers, only the Empire State Building is taller.

Though Wilbur died penniless, Minnesotans will never forget him. To this day the chiseled letters "FOSHAY," 10 feet high and lit by 976 bulbs, are a nighttime beacon.

What the Eiffel Tower is to Paris, the iconic Foshay Tower is to Minneapolis.

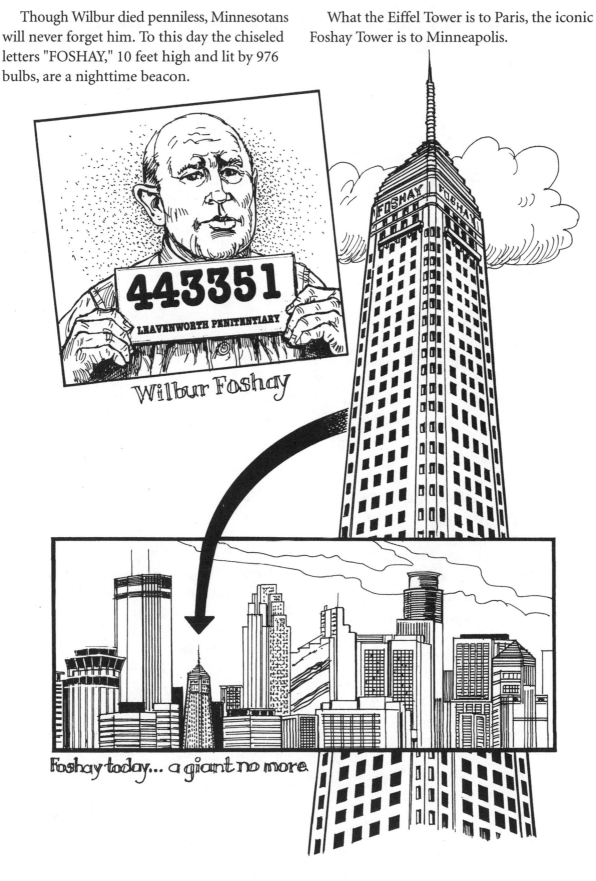

Wilbur Foshay

Foshay today... a giant no more

Doctors Go "Ape" Over First Transplant

America's most charitable state? — The Catalogue for Philanthropy compares "having" to "giving," and ranks Mississippi, perennially last in average income, as the state with the most generous heart.

Speaking of "heart," the world's first heart transplant belongs to the Ole Miss School of Medicine.

In 1955, the School of Medicine at Jackson hired Dr. James Hardy. Although history credits South African surgeon Christiaan Barnhard with the first heart transplant, the Ole Miss School of Medicine's Web site maintains it was Hardy … but with a surprising twist!

By 1963, Hardy was poised to perform the first heart transplant. But this required a donor patient dying at the precise time a recipient needed a heart. The legal concept of "brain dead" hadn't been accepted as a way of establishing suitable donors — one could be declared legally dead only when the heart stopped. Fearing he might never find a human donor under these circumstances, Hardy bought four large chimpanzees. He was influenced by recent chimp-to-human kidney transplants in New Orleans.

In January Hardy had a candidate for a new heart. Hattiesburg resident Boyd Rush, 68, was dying of heart failure. Hardy knew Rush had only hours to live. Fortuitously another person was admitted with a severe brain injury and no prospects of recovery. Hardy assembled his transplant team.

Now came the tricky part: Hardy needed to keep Rush alive until the donor's heart stopped beating. As Rush's blood pressure plunged, Hardy regularly requested updates on the donor's condition. Each time he received the same report: The brain-dead donor's heart was still beating.

Urgently, Hardy faced a great moral question: Should he place an ape's heart in a human's chest? He took the gamble to save Rush's life by removing the heart of Bino, the largest of his chimpanzees. Hardy soon became the first person to peer into an empty but living human chest … and the first to replace one heart with another. Hardy later confided that he wasn't sure the attached chimp heart would start beating on its own. It did.

Technically the transplant was a success. However, Rush lived only two hours with the ape heart. Bino weighed only 96 pounds, making his heart incapable of pumping enough blood through Boyd's larger body.

Other problems surfaced. Was full consent for the weird procedure obtained? Rush, a deaf-mute, entered the hospital in a semi-comatose state. His only known relative, a stepsister, signed a consent form authorizing a "suitable transplant heart" but making no mention of chimpanzees. The stepsister may or may not have been verbally informed of the animal option.

Hardy carefully chose patients on the basis of physical condition and not race (his initial candidate for transplant had been black, while Rush was white). But Mississippi's racial reputation haunted him: Weeks later at the International Transplant Conference in New York, Hardy was humiliated by this opening question from a panel moderator: "In Mississippi, they keep the chimpanzees in one cage and the Negroes in another cage, don't they Dr. Hardy?"

Hardy called the negative reaction to his transplant of a sub-human heart "…a searing experience." He withdrew from the race to perform the first human-to-human heart transplant, won by Barnhard in 1967.

Dr. James Hardy

Bino

Life-or-Death Run Is Legendary

On a river bluff in Missouri is possibly the most understated gravestone in America:

John Colter
Member U.S. Volunteer Mounted Rangers
Mar. 3 – May 6, 1812

Somehow the author of the engraving skipped a few highlights from Colter's life:

First of the Mountain Men
Discoverer of Yellowstone Park
Member, Lewis and Clark Expedition
Survivor of "Colter's Run,"
the most dramatic escape of the Old West

In 1803, Colter caught the eye of a recruiting Meriwether Lewis. Colter jumped at the chance to enlist as a private at the going rate of $5 per month.

Colter served honorably in the expedition. On the return trip, still weeks from St. Louis, the explorers met a pair of frontiersmen bound for present-day Montana to trap beaver. Colter received permission to join them, thus plunging back into the wilderness.

In the coming years, Colter had many close calls, especially with his nemesis the Blackfoot Indians. One encounter is etched in Western lore: The year was 1809. Colter and companion John Potts were checking trap lines by canoe when they were surrounded by hundreds of Blackfeet. Potts was killed in the struggle, and Colter was captured. Initially the warriors seemed intent on using Colter for short-range target practice. But the chief wished to add sport by giving Colter, by now stripped naked and weaponless, a 30-second head start in a foot race for his life.

Colter ran so fast that capillaries in his nose burst, splattering blood on his body. Cactus ripped his feet. After running almost six miles, he had outdistanced all but one of his pursuers.

In desperation, Colter suddenly stopped, turned and threw his arms wide. So startled was the warrior that he tripped, breaking his spear in the fall. Colter grabbed the broken spear and killed his pursuer.

But now more than 100 warriors had closed the gap. Colter sprinted on, reached the Jefferson River and swam under a logjam. There he managed to conceal himself while keeping his nostrils just above water. The irate warriors prowled the banks and even walked directly above Colter's hiding place. When the coast was clear, Colter began a 250-mile, seven-day retreat to his trapper's fort at the mouth of the Bighorn River. Upon arrival he was so bedraggled and starved that comrades couldn't recognize him.

On another trek, Colter discovered today's Yellowstone Park. Others considered his description of geysers and colored hot springs a tall tale. On his last sojourn, Colter returned to find his companions killed by the Blackfeet. He vowed to return to the St. Louis area to buy a small farm and marry Sally.

Colter enjoyed a few quiet years of farming and trapping with his legendary neighbor Daniel Boone. There are conflicting versions of when and how Colter died. He may have died of jaundice, possibly in 1812. In this version Sally, unable to afford a proper burial, left the great explorer "lying in state" on the table of their cabin and went to live with her brother. For the next 114 years the remains lay undisturbed as the cabin slowly crumbled in ruin. In 1926, a steam shovel operator clearing land exposed Colter's bones. These were gathered and buried under the overly modest gravestone on a bluff overlooking his beloved Missouri River.

MISSOURI

DISCOVERING YELLOWSTONE

Unlikely Rescue Rallies Warriors

The "Other Little Big Horn" unfolded at Rosebud Creek, Montana Territory. This all-but-forgotten battle featured General Crook, bound for an 1876 rendezvous with George Custer's 7th Cavalry and other columns. Their plan: Subdue the Cheyenne and Sioux.

Things didn't go as planned. While still a half-day's ride east of Custer, Crook's men were surrounded by an equal force of mounted warriors. Initially pressing the attack, the Indians under Crazy Horse began a slow retreat in the face of superior weaponry. Among the scattered dead and wounded was the Cheyenne warrior Comes-in-Sight.

In the battle's defining moment, Comes-in-Sight's sibling galloped into crossfire to scoop up the wounded brother and carry him to safety. This deliverance from death was so bold that both sides cheered, and the Cheyenne rallied to again press the attack.

The warriors were further emboldened by this curious fact: The rescuer was not a man, but rather Comes-in-Sight's sister Buffalo Calf Road Woman! Only a few Native American tribes allowed the fairer sex into battle. Known as "the manly hearted women," rare female Cheyenne warriors might emerge to avenge the loss of a spouse in battle. But not Buffalo Calf Road Woman, who fought side-by-side with her husband Black Coyote.

Both sides claimed Rosebud victory in what was ultimately a stalemate. The arrow and shell-shocked cavalry was seriously weakened. Crook ordered a southward retreat that prevented his 1,300-man force from joining Custer's 7th Cavalry, thus ensuring the stunning defeat at the Battle of the Little Big Horn one week later.

To historians the contest is remembered as the Battle of the Rosebud — but Indians still call it "The Fight Where the Girl Saved Her Brother."

Buffalo Calf Road Woman wasn't finished — she would become the only woman to fight Custer at the Battle of the Little Big Horn, as told by Rosemary and Joseph Agonito in *Buffalo Calf Road Woman: The Story of a Warrior of the Little Bighorn.*

Shortly *after* this book's 2005 publication, Western historians were stunned by news from Helena, Montana: The Northern Cheyenne called a press conference to break a 129-year vow of silence imposed for fear of retribution after the Little Big Horn Battle. Elders promised to reveal the tribal oral history of what really happened. Controversial and impossible to prove either way, their block-buster revelation was this: Buffalo Calf Road Woman delivered the fatal blow to George Custer, knocking him from his horse just before he died.

The Secret of the Sand Hills

Where would you find the biggest pile of sand in the world? Try the Nebraska Sand Hills, a formation which spills into neighboring Colorado, South Dakota and Kansas and covers 20,000 square miles!

The Sand Hills are actually dunes, each covered by only a few inches of topsoil and a carpet of stabilizing grass.

The Sand Hills are sometimes called America's best managed cattle grasslands. It's true. If over-grazed, Sand Hills grass cover dies, resulting in "blowouts." In these hillside depressions, sand is exposed and relentlessly blown about by the wind.

But the Sand Hills weren't always considered prime cattle country. In 1796, Scotsman James McKay exaggerated somewhat in describing the Sand Hills as, "…a great desert of drifting sand, void of any trees, soil, water or animals of any kind." In the early days of the Open Range, cattlemen steadfastly avoided the Sand Hills, believing the grass to be inferior, and the water scarce.

Then, in the late 1870s a blizzard swept through the Dakotas and scattered thousands of Longhorn cattle southward into the Sand Hills. These distressed animals were given up for lost or dead. But many months later, cowboys chanced upon the missing Longhorns in the heart of the Sand Hills. Not only were they alive, but each had gained more weight than similar cattle outside the Sand Hills. Cattlemen took note, and quickly occupied the Sand Hills with herds as large as 50,000 head.

This ended the myth of poor grass and scarce water. In reality, the Sand Hills are peppered with thousands of lakes and marshes — the sand acts as a huge sponge, collecting the infrequent moisture and creating a high water table and vast underground reservoirs.

And though few know it, this unique region of grass-stabilized dunes contains more grains of sand than the entire Sahara Desert!

Jim Swinehart, a scientist with the University of Nebraska, has asked a disturbing question: What would happen if a prolonged drought, a drought worse than the Dust Bowl of the 1930s, were to occur? Geologists believe that as recently as 900 years ago, the Sand Hills were pure sand — and with no stabilizing grass comes the recurring period called "dune time," a time when winds cause the lifeless dunes to march slowly across the land. Though Swinehart will not predict when "dune time" will come again, he's sure another super drought will one day set the vast ocean of sand in motion.

Student Mistakenly Kills Oldest Living Thing

America is home to the world's biggest tree, tallest tree and oldest tree.

But that "oldest" claim was unknown until 1957, when Dr. Edmund Schulman discovered a ghost-like grove of bristlecone pines — trees that had survived for 4,000 years perched high in the White Mountains above California's Mojave Desert.

What Schulman discovered about tree longevity stunned the scientific world: Ironically, the oldest trees invariably grow in the worst conditions — high altitude sites with scant soil and moisture. This is because for trees, slower growth means longer life. Old bristlecone pines are masters of slow growth, adding just 1/100th of an inch to girth size annually. And because other trees and forbs can't survive in such harsh conditions, the bristlecone is free of plant competitors — and therefore free from the threat of fire.

Following Schulman's discovery, a band of Nevada naturalists championed a grove of colossal bristlecones on the flank of 13,063-foot Wheeler Peak near Nevada's eastern border with Utah. The group's leader was naturalist Darwin Lambert, who dreamed of national park status for his beloved trees and mountain.

Because California's bristlecones were assumed to be the world's oldest trees, they garnered the media attention. In response, Lambert raised the distinct possibility that Nevada's Wheeler Peak bristecones were equally as old as those in California. Lambert and his pals bestowed fanciful names on their favorite bristlecones, like "Socrates" and "Buddha." One tree was named after "Prometheus," the Greek god who gifted mankind with fire and the arts, thus earning the punishment of being chained to a mountain for thousands of years.

Year after year, Lambert supported congressional legislation to create a Great Basin National Park. Year after year, mining and grazing interests intervened to thwart the legislation.

One day in 1964, University of Nevada student Donald Currey drove to Wheeler Peak as part of his search for evidence of Ice Age glaciers in the Southwest. Currey and fellow students climbed up to Wheeler Peak's tree line, where they came upon the ancient pines. They began taking core samples to determine ancient weather patterns based on tree-ring width. (A coring tool allows researchers to extract a bead of wood for counting and comparing rings without harming the tree.) They were excited to find one tree with more than 4,000 annual rings.

During his investigation Currey's only coring tool became stuck in a tree. Currey sought permission from the Forest Service to cut down the tree to retrieve the tool. Inexplicably, permission was granted.

So down came the ancient timber, which turned out to be "Prometheus." When the students gathered around the fresh stump, they counted 4,862 rings. Oops! Young Mr. Currey had just killed the oldest living thing on Earth.

Was this the biggest "oops" in scientific history? Or would these words of a colleague of Darwin Lambert prove more important — and ultimately prophetic: "'Prometheus might become widely enough known as a martyr to save the other ancients."

Indeed, this "martyr tree" incident brought more stringent protection to the Wheeler Peak bristlecones. Within years, the 77,000-acre Great Basin National Park was established around that stump of old "Prometheus."

Mysteries Shroud "America's Stonehenge"

The New Hampshire hills hold evidence of a vanished people who used muscle and lever to move massive stones together to form "America's Stonehenge." This puzzling monument was first known as Mystery Hill — and for good reasons.

Located near Salem, N. H., Mystery Hill is 20 acres of stone structures vaguely reminiscent of the megalithic landmarks of Western Europe. Some have suggested Mystery Hill is evidence of an ancient culture, possibly even Bronze Age Europeans.

Others dismiss Mystery Hill as the work of early colonialists in need of root cellars and sheep shelters. This explanation conflicts with the dating of tree roots intertwined with rock walls, indicating building dates preceding the area's first European settlement. Additionally, carbon 14 analysis of charcoal found beside the structures reveals campfires thought to be 4,000 years old.

Adding another layer of mystery are scattered man-made inscriptions on the stones, which the late author Barry Fell believed to be Phoenician or Iberian Punic script. Fell conducted extensive research on the inscriptions, even proposing translations revealed in his controversial book *America B.C.* Pillars of stone form a great circle around the complex in seemingly mystical alignment to the sun and moon — an apparent giant astronomy calendar.

When former insurance agent William Goodwin bought the property in 1936, his pet theory was that ninth-century Irish monks built the structures. Goodwin proved overly enthusiastic, however, for we now know he freely moved stones around to better fit his theory.

Even before Goodwin, the evidence at Mystery Hill was greatly altered by demand for building stones in nearby Massachusetts towns. In the 1920s an estimated 20 percent to 50 percent of Mystery Hill's original stones were carted off to urban construction sites.

Thus, today's Mystery Hill is a faint echo of what once was. But some intact elements survive, such as the puzzling "Oracle Chamber." This underground chamber at the heart of the complex contains a stone-lined shaft, the so-called "Speaking Tube." The tube emerges above ground but it's concealed under a four-ton stone sacrificial altar. A shaman hidden in the Oracle Chamber could talk into the tube, his voice amplified and carried up to the altar above. In theory this would have impressed or deceived worshippers gathered around the altar.

With its astronomical alignments, and chambers often too small to be practical storage units, Mystery Hill has the look of a ceremonial site. But could it really be of Celtic, Viking or Phoenician origin? Such theories await further evidence as researchers search for the conspicuously absent artifacts that could confirm a link to early European cultures.

Alternately, if Mystery Hill is the work of Indians, where was the technology needed to move the great stones weighing four to 11 tons each? Known Native Americans of New England exhibited little interest in hewn-rock building techniques.

This is the riddle without an answer that was set to verse in 1900 by poet Thomas Higginson. Here are excerpts from *An American Stonehenge:*

"Far up on these abandoned mountain farms
Now drifting back to forest wilds again,
The long, gray walls extend their clasping arms,
Pathetic monument of vanished men.

Nearer than stones of storied Saxon name
These speechless relics to our hearts should come."

Suffrage Struggle Spans 150 Years

There was a little-known corner of Colonial America where women could vote, but not if they chose to marry!

When the founding fathers met in Philadelphia to frame the U.S. Constitution, they deferred voter qualifications to the states. Immediately, women lost the right to vote in every state but one. Only New Jersey chose to preserve a state constitution (circa 1776) granting voting rights to "all inhabitants" regardless of gender or race.

For the next 20 years, women of New Jersey — and only New Jersey — could vote. But there was a catch: Voting was restricted to persons who owned at least $250 in property. Because married women couldn't own property, effectively only single women and widows could vote.

Alas, New Jersey women, along with "aliens and Negros," lost the vote in 1807. After the Civil War, Wyoming Territory falsely claimed to be the first state/territory to grant women the vote. In 1870, federal politicians pressured Utah officials to grant women's suffrage in the belief that, given the vote, Utah women would surely reject polygamy. But when females in the future Beehive State consistently voted *in favor* of polygamy, Congress promptly disenfranchised Utah women.

The battle for women's suffrage was a series of small victories. For example, women were often allowed to vote exclusively in school board elections. Finally, in 1920, American women gained full voting rights with the 19th Amendment's ratification.

Though New Jersey was first under the U.S. Constitution to allow women's suffrage, Colorado was the first state to give women the vote via a male-only election. The year was 1893, and organizers won in Colorado using this amusing but effective campaign slogan: "Let the women vote! They can't do any worse than the men!"

Unlikely Tennessee also played a role in advancing women's suffrage. It happened after Congress passed the 19th Amendment but before the required 36 states had ratified. There was a sense of urgency when several states (Georgia, Alabama, South Carolina, Virginia, Maryland, Mississippi, Delaware and Louisiana) actually rejected the amendment. Thirty-five had approved, but would there be a 36th?

That's when Tennessee's House of Representatives twice voted the amendment to a dead-heat tie. On the third ballot, Republican legislator Harry T. Burn of Niota bravely switched his vote, and the 19th Amendment instantly became the law of the land.

In 1988, one Tennessee city government drew national and international attention by electing an all-woman commission, making it the only exclusively female municipal government in America. Coincidentally or not, this municipality was Niota, the hometown of Harry T. Burn!

Canyon Hides Prehistoric Riddles

Chaco Canyon in hard-scrabble northwest New Mexico is an unlikely place for the cultural capital of a 40,000-square-mile empire. This center for the Ancestral Pueblo (Anasazi) people was the supreme architectural achievement of prehistoric North America. Its crowning jewel was Pueblo Bonita, a massive "great house" of 667 rooms covering three acres. Archeologists have recently solved three of Pueblo Bonita's four strangest riddles:

Riddle #1—One might anticipate a 667-room structure to be home to at least 1,500 souls. But based on the number of fire pits and burials, scientists say Pueblo Bonita was home to just 20 families! Why all those rooms? Pueblo Bonita was "public architecture," built to impress friend and foe, and to host periodic gatherings for ceremonies and commerce. Trade items included live parrots and macaws, seashells, and copper bells from as far away as the tropics.

Riddle #2—We know that construction at Chaco Canyon required 220,000 ponderosa pine trees. We also know that for the past 10,000 years there have been no pine forests closer to arid Chaco Canyon than the Chuska Mountains, which are more than 50 miles away. The largest logs were ceiling supports 27 inches in diameter, 14 feet tall, and weighing more than one ton each when cut.

How then did a people with neither beasts of burden nor the wheel transport such logs more than 50 miles? Could they have dragged the logs? No, because not one timber bears longitudinal scars from being dragged overland. Could the logs have been floated to Chaco during rare flash floods? No, since the logs lack compression bruises consistent with floating down rocky streams. What's the answer? — Ancient workmen using stone axes peeled the bark, and then left the logs to dry for up to two years. Less moisture meant less weight allowing many men paired off with hide straps to carry each great log all the way to Chaco.

Riddle #3—Carrying the logs was easier thanks to an elaborate system of roads radiating from Chaco Canyon. The roads themselves are a mystery, each precisely 30-feet-wide and engineered straight as an arrow, regardless of terrain. Where obstacles were encountered, the roads were terraced, ramped or included steps carved in solid rock. Sometimes these rock stairways ended at sheer cliffs, which leads to the third riddle:

Did the pedestrian Chacoans really need such wide, often redundantly parallel roads? And why were roads so stubbornly straight that they might end with chiseled steps leading over a cliff? What's the answer? Like the great houses, roads were more ceremonial than practical. The pharaohs of old used pyramid construction to give purpose and structure to Egyptian society; just as Chacoan leaders used road building to instill societal and religious discipline in subjects.

For the unsolved fourth riddle, turn the page. (Note: Aerial traces of the roads, such as one leading directly north from the canyon, are clearly visible at www.googleearth.com.)

Pueblo
Bonito

Ancients Tempt Fate at Leaning "Tower"

With dozens of miles of canyon from which to choose, why would the Ancestral Pueblo (Anasazi) people of famed Chaco Canyon build their defining structure in the ominous shadow of Threatening Rock?

In 850 A.D., construction on splendid Pueblo Bonita began beneath this rock colossus, which then looked even more menacing because the valley floor was an estimated 15 feet lower. Threatening Rock, all 30,000 tons of it, towered 113 feet high and 130 feet wide. To modern eyes, it would resemble an 11-story building tilted like Italy's Leaning Tower of Pisa.

We know Chacoans recognized the threat, as they built elaborate retaining walls around the base of Threatening Rock in hopes of propping up the monolith and slowing erosion.

For 300 years the Chacoans continued to add rooms to five-story Pueblo Bonito. Then came a day in 1140 A.D. when the pueblo's 667th and final room was finished, and its people mysteriously abandoned the canyon. Into this now empty land the Navajo tribe migrated.

When the National Park Service assumed Chaco Canyon's administration in 1907, Threatening Rock had already loomed over Pueblo Bonita for more than a millennium. A park service custodian began monitoring the rock's tilt, and noted the gap between the cliff was widening 1-2 inches each year.

The winter of 1940-41 was unusually rainy. On Jan. 22, Threatening Rock came crashing down, exploding into house-sized boulders and destroying a portion of Pueblo Bonita. A 50-year-old Navajo, sharing the belief of fellow tribesmen that the world would end when the rock came down, crouched in his nearby tent and cried.

Threatening Rock was gone. All that remained was the enigma of why Chacoans chose to build there. Researchers combed the rubble for clues, and found ancient prayer sticks in the crevice between the rock and cliff. Called "pahos," these carved and painted willow wands decorated with feathers are still offered by Pueblo people in a manner similar to how altar candles are used.

The pahos suggest that living beneath Threatening Rock was a gesture of faith in the Great Spirit. There are other clues, such as the traditional Navajo legend that Chaco Canyon was home to the mythical Great Gambler.

Perhaps fittingly, the full answer to this mystery died with the ancients. But if indeed Pueblo Bonita's placement had something to do with faith, such faith wasn't misplaced. After all, Threatening Rock stood strong for 1,100 years!

When Texans Dropped the A-Bomb…on Albuquerque!

Residents of Albuquerque, N.M. always knew that if the Cold War turned "hot," their city's proximity to nuclear facilities at Los Alamos, Sandia and Kirtland Air Force Base would make them a prime Soviet target.

This made the events of 1957 such a shock to the few who knew the truth, for on May 22 a large silver aircraft dropped an atomic bomb on U.S. soil, just south of Albuquerque. The crew members weren't Russian, but Texan — airmen from Biggs Air Force Base near El Paso and bound for Kirtland.

The bomb's release was an accident. The conventional explosives of the 42,000 lb. armament detonated, but luckily didn't start a nuclear chain reaction. Regardless, the explosion carved a 25-foot-wide crater. The lone casualty was a luckless New Mexico cow grazing nearby.

Code-named the Mark 17, this bomb was the mother of all bombs. At 25-feet long, it was the largest thermonuclear weapon of that era — 700 times more powerful than the bomb dropped on Hiroshima.

The plane's radio operator, George Houston, alertly responded with a distress call to the nearby Kirtland control tower. Stunned air traffic controllers listened as he reported the unthinkable: "We've dropped a hydrogen bomb."

The Special Weapons Project staff quickly and quietly conducted recovery/cleanup operations. The moderate radiation detected was confined to the crater. As with virtually all nuclear weapons, the Mark 17 was designed to detonate only with a remotely controlled trigger device — never on impact.

The day when America bombed America wasn't officially acknowledged by the Defense Department until a 1980 thumbnail description of the event appeared in a larger report on nuclear weapons accidents. Six years later, reporters from the *Albuquerque Journal* used the Freedom of Information Act to provide curious citizens with the full story.

More than 50 years after the accident, New Mexicans with ordinary metal detectors and Geiger counters still find small pieces of the original bomb. Some debris is as far as one mile from the crash site, and each retains a low level of detectable radioactivity.

So you think this is all very interesting, but not relevant to your home state? Whoa, not so fast! Turn to page 126 to see how close Doomsday came to your backyard.

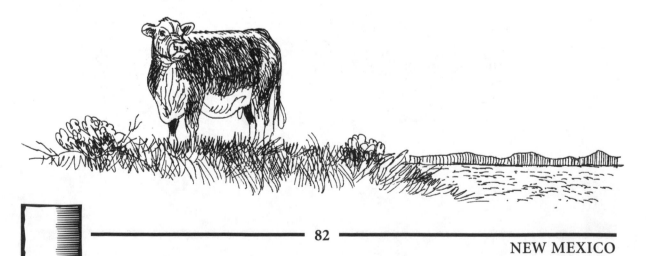

Draft Loophole Ignites Riots

In 1863, Abe Lincoln signed a bill authorizing America's first national military draft (in earlier wars the states held this power). Wealthy men facing Civil War battlefields, however, enjoyed a major loophole: It was perfectly legal for well-feathered draftees to either hire a substitute soldier or pay the government $300 for automatic commutation. As a result, the Civil War was popularly known as "the rich man's war and the poor man's fight."

Middle-class northerners formed clubs whereby if one club member was drafted, the others would chip in to pay either his substitute or his commutation fee. In some Union counties, taxes were raised or raffles held to pay substitutes so that residents of those counties need not fight. An estimated 6 percent of Yankee soldiers, nearly 130,000 men, were actually paid substitutes.

This unfairness contributed to the New York City draft riots of July 1863. Commerce in the city came to a halt during the riots, as insurgents set dozens of buildings ablaze, including the mayor's residence on the site of today's Madison Square Garden. Certain newspapers incited the Irish working class to riot by criticizing the federal government's draft law as a tool of what they called the "nigger war."

Blacks became targets of the rioter's anger — they weren't considered citizens, so they were exempt from the draft. Several adults and even some children among the "coloreds" were hunted down and lynched or clubbed to death.

Still, there were a few examples of interracial cooperation. When rioters threatened black drugstore owner Philip White, his Irish neighbors drove the mob away, for he had often extended them credit.

For days, the city teetered on the brink of anarchy. An estimated 110 people died. News that the draft was being suspended eased tensions, as did martial law enforced by thousands of federal troops arriving directly from the recent Battle of Gettysburg.

The riot and the flawed conscription law would haunt the Empire State for decades. Even former New York Governor Theodore Roosevelt, America's "Bull Moose" president and a volunteer military leader and hero of the Spanish-American War, faced repeated questions on a "skeleton" from his family closet. Teddy's father, Theodore Roosevelt Sr., had sidestepped the Civil War by paying a substitute soldier to take his place in battle.

The same can be said for the future governor of New York and president of the United States, Grover Cleveland, who in 1863 paid Polish immigrant George Benninsky $150 to be his Civil War substitute.

The Story of America's "Anne Frank"

The most curiously overlooked great American heroine may have been Harriet Jacobs, North Carolina's fugitive slave, author and activist.

When the orphan Harriet was 12, her slave-owning mistress died. The will declared Harriet the property of a 5-year-old niece of the deceased mistress. But Harriet's de facto master would be the 5-year-old's father, Dr. James Norcom. When she reached a certain age, this master commenced sexual harassment that became ever worse. Norcom wouldn't let Jacobs marry, though she had two children by consensual lover Samuel Sawyer.

Being a slave, Jacobs had no recourse to Norcom's crimes. Fearing he might sell her children to a distant slave owner, she resolved to flee to the North. When that proved impossible, in 1835 Jacobs entered hiding in a tiny garret above her grandmother's nearby home. She wouldn't emerge for seven years, though the attic had no source of light or fresh air and measured just 9 feet by 7 feet with a sloping roof three feet tall at the highest point. Before hiding, Jacobs entrusted her children to her grandmother. She dared not divulge her hiding place to even her offspring, knowing Norcom would coerce them for information.

Jacobs' sole source of light and joy in those years was a hole she drilled in the attic sidewall. This wee window on the world allowed her to see the faces and hear the voices of her children. In later writings she confessed the near impossibility of stifling the urge to shout, "I am here!"

Sensory deprivation eventually led to hallucinations. Yet Harriet persevered, even finding fun at Norcom's expense by writing him letters, then smuggling the letters to New York to be postmarked. This duped the doctor into fruitless trips north to retrieve his fugitive slave.

In 1842, Jacobs accepted passage on a ship bound for freedom. She masqueraded as a sailor for the walk down to the harbor — a less-than-convincing disguise because her limbs were atrophied from seven years of inactivity. The ship sailed to New York City, where she found jobs necessary to eventually buy her children's freedom.

Jacobs' autobiography, the first slave narrative from a woman's perspective, appeared initially in Horace Greeley's *New York Tribune*. But when she sought a book publisher, there were not takers — "too shocking" said their rejections. Indeed, her manifesto pulled no punches, exposing the heretofore hidden sexuality of slavery whereby defenseless female slaves became virtual "sex slaves."

Finally, at the onset of the Civil War, Jacobs found a publisher for her *Incidents in the Life of a Slave Girl*. It was the book, says scholar William Andrews, that made Jacobs "…the most important African-American woman writer of the 19th century." Celebrated female ex-slaves Sojourner Truth and Harriet Tubman were illiterate. Literacy among slaves was then against the law. Because Jacobs was literate, hers is the only surviving voice for those millions.

And she was just getting started! Jacobs spent the war spearheading medical relief behind Union lines. She founded the Jacobs Free School, America's first institution to provide black teachers for refugee slaves. At war's end, Jacobs relocated to Savannah, Ga., to continue relief work. By 1868, anti-black violence in the South forced a retreat to Massachusetts, where Jacobs lectured and advocated for the "coloreds" until her death.

NORTH CAROLINA

Though now largely forgotten, the images of persecution and a life in hiding in *"Incidents"* make it the uniquely American equivalent of *"The Diary of Anne Frank."*

$100 REWARD

W ILL be given for the apprehension and delivery of my Servant Girl HARRIET. She is light mulatto, 21 years of age, 5 feet 4 inches high, of a thick and bit, having on her head a ...ir that curls nat... ...mbed st...

Poker Jim Plays the "Dead Man's Hand"

Teddy Roosevelt was a genuine North Dakota cowboy. But he was hardly the most colorful. That title goes to Poker Jim, a Badlands cowhand and ruffian who loved poker so much that he literally dropped in on a game after his death!

Poker Jim's real name remains a mystery. That may be just the way he liked it, because Poker Jim was presumably an outlaw who had drifted up to North Dakota's Badlands on one of the last great cattle drives. Up north Jim found work with the enormous W-Bar Ranch. When not working cattle, Jim could be found playing in frontier poker games —and usually winning.

Then came the bitterly cold winter of 1894, when Poker Jim and a companion were stationed at a remote cow camp near the Little Missouri River. By February their food supply was critically low, and Jim drew the short straw when deciding who would ride 70 miles to Glendive, Mont. for fresh supplies.

But Jim never made it. One week later, cowboys found Jim's frozen body propped against a rock near a creek 10 miles from camp.

Jim's horse was tied to a tree, and though still alive, it had desperately stripped and consumed much of the tree's bark. Burned matches near Jim's body indicated that he had tried vainly to build a fire.

Those who found Poker Jim's frozen body carried it to an abandoned shack some distance away. To foil scavenging wolves and provide a sort of "cold storage," they hoisted the stiff corpse into the rafters. Then they left.

The Feb. 24, 1973 edition of the *Minot* (ND) *Daily News* describes what happened next:

"Later another group of men gathered at the shack for a poker game. They heated the building, and the body (unbeknownst to them) gradually thawed. Finally it fell right onto the poker table directly below. According to the tale, no poker game ever broke up so fast."

And so it was that Jim posthumously participated in one last poker game. He was buried in a rural Badlands hilltop cemetery now named after one of America's least-known, but most colorful cowboys: Poker Jim.

Poet's Words Take Flight

He was born Paul Laurence Dunbar in 1872 to former slaves. Dunbar's mother Matilda worked as a domestic for a white family in Dayton, Ohio, and it was there that he first met Orville. They ended up in the same class at Central High School. Their friendship was one for the Ages.

Though Paul was the only person of color in his class, he was editor-in-chief of the school newspaper and eventually became president of the senior class. Orville dropped out of high school. In an era when interracial friendships were frowned on, they became lifelong comrades. Orville, who loved to tinker, built a printing press. It was on this press that the two jointly published the ethnic newspaper *The Dayton Tattler.*

Dunbar soon gained fame in the literary world. He recited poetry at the Chicago World's Fair and read to adoring crowds in Europe. Frederick Douglass declared Dunbar, "the most promising young black man in America."

Yet Dunbar's health was not good. When scheduled to read his poems and novels before a huge hometown Dayton crowd, including old friend Orville, Dunbar's health suddenly worsened. He couldn't even climb to the podium, so the event was canceled.

Paul Laurence Dunbar died soon after. He was just 33. In failing health, Dunbar had returned to his mother's home where he wrote until the end. After his death, Matilda lovingly kept his small study unchanged as a shrine for visiting fans. This included the page containing his final unfinished poem, positioned precisely as he had left it on his desk. When Matilda died, it was discovered that the sun had bleached the ink, so this last poem was lost forever.

Yet many of Dunbar's poems survive. Some reflect the racism he faced in life, including these lines from what is perhaps his most famous poem, "We Wear the Mask":

We wear the mask that grins and lies,
It hides our cheeks and shades our eyes,—
This debt we pay to human guile;
With torn and bleeding hearts we smile,
And mouth with myriad subtleties.

Or consider this prophetic early ode to a caged bird in "Sympathy," which may echo his ties with Orville:

I know why the caged bird sings, ah me,
    When his wing is bruised and his bosom sore,-
When he beats his bars and he would be free:
It is not a carol of joy or glee,
    But a prayer that he sends from his heart's deep core,
But a plea, that upward to Heaven he flings-
I know why the caged bird sings.

A "caged bird" in all of us was set free two years before Dunbar's untimely death when lifelong friend and high school dropout Orville Wright of the Wright brothers invented and piloted man's first airplane. The tombstones of the schoolmates are not far apart in the same Dayton cemetery … a fitting end to Ohio's proudest friendship.

OHIO

I know why the caged bird sings, a
When his wing is bruised and h
When he beats his bars and he w
It is not a carol of joy or glee,
But a prayer that he sends
But a plea, that upward to
I bird

Indians Saddle Up for Rebel Cause

Europeans colonizing the East Coast used various techniques to subjugate the Native Americans. The combined effects of warfare, disease and enslavement wiped out entire tribes.

Five southern tribes survived this early colonial period by adopting Anglo-European lifestyles. The Cherokee, Choctaw, Chickasaw, Creek and Seminole — known as the "Civilized Tribes" — mimicked whites in dress, livelihood, education, and among mixed-bloods even the ownership of black slaves.

"Civilized" or not, President Andrew Jackson wished to remove all Southern tribes to west of the Mississippi in a newly designated "Indian Territory," which today we call Oklahoma.

What followed was a forced march infamously known as the "Trail of Tears." Tribal members brought their personal property — household items, livestock, and nearly 15,000 enslaved blacks.

Arriving in Indian Territory was Stand Watie, a mixed-blood Cherokee farmer and slave owner. Watie, like many others, resented the broken promises of the U.S. government. Thus, when America entered its Civil War, Watie and other Indians eagerly renounced treaties with the Union and aligned themselves with the Confederacy.

Yet many in the Civilized Tribes retained Northern sympathies. This blood feud resulted in competing governments for the Cherokee Nation. Stand Watie was named chief executive of the Confederate Cherokee Nation.

Watie formed a rebel cavalry of Cherokee and Creek warriors. He daringly led them into many battles — victories such as Wilson's Creek, and defeats such as Pea Ridge. Watie also ruthlessly raided across Indian Territory, killing fellow Cherokees suspected of Union leanings. He was the only Indian general of the Confederacy.

No jurisdiction suffered a higher Civil War casualty rate than Indian Territory. Despite the deadly chaos, Watie and his fellow officers tried to carry on the functions of government by holding legislative sessions and enacting laws under a military tent.

At war's end, Watie and other Confederate Indians were forced to accept the terms of the 1866 Treaty, which required tribes to free black slaves and accept them into tribal membership. Northern "carpetbaggers" justified the unilateral terms of the Treaty because some of Watie's Confederate Indian cavalry had scalped Union soldiers at Pea Ridge.

Watie had the distinction of being the last Confederate general to surrender, nearly three months after Robert E. Lee offered his sword at Appomattox. Such was the slow nature of military communications. Even after Watie laid down his arms, one band of rebel sailors kept fighting. Unaware that the war was over, the warship Shenandoah had sailed to the Bering Sea to battle the Union whaling fleet.

Finally on June 28, 1865, the Shenandoah's gunner aimed, jerked a lanyard, and fired the last shot of the American Civil War.

Pals Launch Enterprise with a "Swoosh"

In the 1960s, Oregonians Bill Bowerman and Phil Knight founded a tiny athletic company called Blue Ribbon Sports. Their first retail outlet was the back of Knight's car, parked conspicuously at high school track meets.

Bowerman invented the modern running shoe, Blue Ribbon's waffle-soled shoe, after experimenting with liquid rubber poured into his wife's waffle iron. Later the company was re-named for the Greek goddess of victory: Nike.

While coaching the track team at the University of Oregon, Bowerman heavily recruited a scrawny but promising youth from nearby Coos Bay.

Long-haired and free-spirited, this teen runner originally wanted to play football, for which he was much too small. With one leg longer than the other, he was also advised to give up his new dream – to become the faster runner in the world. As rebellious as he was obsessed, Steve Prefontaine wouldn't be denied. "Pre" would rise to iconic status in Oregon, the only region of America where track stars are treated like rock stars.

Prefontaine turned running into a blood sport with his aggressive "front running" style. He ultimately held every U.S. track record from 2,000 meters to 10,000 meters.

The sports world will never know what heights he might have gained, as Prefontaine died tragically in an auto accident at age 24. Death vaulted him to James Dean-like sainthood among runners. Movies and books followed. ESPN writer Jeff Merron declared Prefontaine the most popular American runner of all time.

Knight and Bowerman had employed Prefontaine as a Nike ambassador and the first athlete to endorse a running shoe. After Pre's death, the next paid Nike sports personality would be basketball superstar Michael Jordan. In those early days, Nike couldn't support co-founder Phil Knight. He took a job teaching accounting at Portland State, where he met student graphic artist Carolyn Davidson. Knight asked Davidson to try creating a logo, one that would in his words, "suggest movement." Davidson charged Knight $35 to create the legendary Nike "Swoosh" logo. It became one of the world's most recognizable logos, surpassed only by McDonald's golden arches on some continents.

Years later, the logo Davidson sold for just $35 would be valued by Interbrand's Most Valuable Brands survey at $3.015 billion!

Phil Knight

Bill Bowerman

USA

Steve Prefontaine

Unearthly Fire Dooms Town

Fire, the great mystery, is even more mysterious when burning in the underworld. Pennsylvania leads the nation in subterranean conflagrations.

One of America's earliest written descriptions of underground fire is from the Lewis and Clark Expedition, a transcontinental trek launched from Pittsburgh in 1803. The following year, expedition members reported a curious phenomenon known as "burning bluffs" along the Missouri River in present-day South Dakota. Apparently ignited by spontaneous combustion, organic oils in the cliffs smolder and smoke but exhibit no visible flames. Meriwether Lewis was duly impressed.

Back in Pennsylvania, underground fires later reduced one town of 2,000 souls to "ghost town" status. It all started in 1962, when local volunteer firemen from Centralia, Pa. were burning trash at a dump near the cemetery. Their mission: to reduce odors before Memorial Day.

As usual, they hosed down the flames when finished. But this time, smoldering trash dropped through a hole into abandoned coal mine tunnels zigzagging beneath the town. A coal fire ignited that has burned for nearly 50 years.

At first the fire was a mere curiosity. Smoke curled from cracks in the cemetery turf. Kathy Gabinski remembers harvesting tomatoes at Christmas, thanks to her year-round toasty garden soil. Residents no longer had to shovel snow.

But when the main highway through town dropped eight feet, it was the start of real troubles. Some Centralians began passing out in their homes from carbon monoxide seeping into basements. Next, an underground gas tank down at the Esso gas station heated up to a dangerous 172 degrees.

By 1982, people were deserting Centralia in droves. That's the year 12-year-old Todd Domboski was running across a neighbor's backyard when suddenly a 150-foot-deep hole opened under his feet. Domboski fell into a haze of poison gas and smoke, but saved himself by grabbing an exposed tree root. A cousin pulled him to safety.

Workers have battled the hellish Centralia fire for decades, alternately flushing the mine shafts with water and ash, drilling, setting backfires and trenching in heroic but futile fashion. Coal mine fires are notoriously difficult to extinguish. Presently the Centralia fire isn't being fought. Some experts predict the fire will expand to 2,700 acres, threaten the nearby town of Ashland, and burn for 300 years. (This is small potatoes compared to Australia's Burning Mountain — scientists believe this oldest-known coal fire has burned nonstop for 6,000 years.)

In 1992, the Commonwealth of Pennsylvania condemned all buildings in Centralia, and over 600 were demolished. Most residents accepted government buyout offers. But nine residents remain in Centralia — holdouts living as squatters in their own homes. Officials are reluctant to evict them.

Former residents still make the risky trip back to Centralia — some for weekly Saturday services in the one remaining church — others to tend graves in 140-year-old St. Ignatius Cemetery.

To its credit, the town that lost nearly everything never did lose its sense of humor. One local joke says that only in Centralia can you get buried and cremated at the same time, no extra charge.

Smallest State Takes Biggest Stand for Liberty

Our smallest state came up big in the fight to guarantee freedom of religion for every American. Here's how:

The founder of Rhode Island, Roger Williams, was born in Shakespearian England. As a young boy he lived in London's Smithfield neighborhood near a plaza where Puritans and other religious nonconformists were routinely burned at the stake. Such intolerance no doubt influenced young Williams' later belief in a separation of church and state, and may have provoked him to set sail for the New World.

In 1631, Williams began preaching to congregations at Plymouth and Salem on Massachusetts Bay, where his free thinking soon set him at odds with civil and religious authorities. For example, Williams opposed a local tradition allowing Europeans to take land from Indians without compensation. When the outspoken Williams was banished and scheduled to be forcibly returned to England, he instead moved in with Indian friends. Months later, he purchased native lands for a new colony in what's now Rhode Island. To show his gratitude to God, Williams named his new capital "Providence."

From the beginning, Rhode Island opened its doors to persons of any faith, or no faith at all. Among the first to accept the invitation was the unauthorized Puritan minister Anne Hathaway, followed by Quakers and other so-called heretics. In the mid 1600s, Jews fleeing the Spanish inquisition arrived and established the oldest synagogue in the Western Hemisphere.

Many of America's first colonists left Europe for religious freedom, only to later deny that same freedom to others. Not Roger Williams. Only in his Rhode Island did the seed of religious freedom grow into a sturdy tree. Many believe Thomas Jefferson's "wall of separation between church and state" was inspired by the pen of Roger Williams a full 150 years earlier.

Which leads us to the sometimes ambivalent status of the Christian faith among our Founding Fathers: Thomas Jefferson, John Adams, Ben Franklin, James Madison and Thomas Paine are sometimes referred to as deists. Deism is the belief that a benevolent God created this Universe, but subsequently had little daily involvement in the affairs of man. Deists were skeptical of miracles, and some even questioned the divinity of Christ. Jefferson, for example, kept his own version of the four Gospels in which miracles were meticulously cut out with a razor.

Jefferson refused to discuss his religious beliefs, leading many to believe he was an atheist. When Jefferson was elected president, some believers hid their Bibles to avoid seizure by "the satanic Jefferson."

In fact, Jefferson was religious and did attend church, as did most of the Founding Fathers. Though their spiritual views might be considered eccentric in modern-day America, the deists seemed to envision a tolerant yet faithful nation. After all, they signed a Declaration of Independence with a preamble containing these words:

"All men … are endowed by their Creator with certain unalienable rights …."

Turn the page to see how petite Rhode Island yet again stood tall for religious freedom.

Thomas
Jefferson

Bde Crawford

In God They Trusted — Sometimes

Inspired by founder Roger Williams, Rhode Island always has been a haven for religious freedom.

Rhode Island's government neutrality in matters of faith affected even the U.S. Constitution. Recalcitrant little "Rhodie" would be the last of the original 13 colonies to ratify the Constitution, holding out for a Bill of Rights. The state's leaders got their wish after agreeing to ratify the Constitution – a Bill of Rights was added with the famous First Amendment: "Congress shall make no law respecting an establishment of religion."

Regardless, the framers and legislators of America have struggled to maintain a secular government without being perceived as godless.

The motto "In God We Trust" was first placed on U. S. coins because of increased religious sentiment during the savage Civil War. The same motto wouldn't appear on U.S. paper money until 1957.

Opposition to the motto came from an unlikely source: Republican Theodore Roosevelt, a devout Christian, believed the words to be unconstitutional in that they promote a state religion in opposition to the First Amendment. He also believed putting the name of God on money was a sacrilege. In Roosevelt's own words, "…it seems to me eminently unwise to cheapen such a motto by use on coins, just as it would be to cheapen it by use on postage stamps, or in advertisements."

In 1796, a young Andrew Jackson, delegate to Tennessee's statehood convention, used similar reasoning in opposing inclusion of the term "God" in the state constitution.

The American judiciary has been somewhat ambivalent on these topics. The Ninth Circuit Court of Appeals once ruled that "under God" couldn't be recited in the Pledge of Allegiance. That ruling was eventually overturned. A little-known fact is that the Pledge of Allegiance was written by an American Socialist, Francis Bellamy. Bellamy penned the Pledge in his career as a writer after being pressured to resign a Boston Baptist church because of his socialist sermons.

The words "under God" were subsequently added to the Pledge during the anti-Communist fervor of the 1950s.

Late in life, James Madison reflected on the Founding Fathers' thoughts on religion. He wrote that houses of worship and governments are each kept most pure when we prohibit one from meddling in the affairs of the other. The author of this logic, Roger Williams, had died in the distant past, buried at home in his beloved Rhode Island.

Nearly 253 years after his burial, Williams' remains were to be moved to a bronze container at the base of a monument in Providence. In that year, 1936, his remains were uncovered for reburial from under an apple tree. Over the decades the roots of this tree grew into the spot where Williams' formidable brain had once rested, and from there followed the path of the decomposing bones — growing in roughly the shape of his skeleton. So while there would be scarcely any of the Williams remains to venerate, there is the bizarre "Williams Root," which to this day is part of the collection of the Rhode Island Historical Society.

Williams Root

Francis
Bellamy

The Strange Story of Human Bondage

Slavery was *not* introduced to the New World by Europeans. Most Native American tribes practiced some form of human bondage long before traders brought kidnapped Africans to America.

Aboriginal slavery was, however, a different institution — Indian slaves were usually war captives allowed to live relatively free lives on the fringes of society. Often children born to slaves were considered full tribal member. Regardless, Indian slaves might suffer amputation of a foot to discourage escape, or ritual murder to avenge the death of a tribe's warrior.

When Europeans arrived, the sometimes benevolent nature of indigenous slavery changed. Early British colonists eagerly purchased slaves from those tribes willing to sell, especially in present-day South Carolina. Unscrupulous traders encouraged Indians to make war on neighboring tribes, knowing they would reap profits from battlefield enslavements. Before the hey-day of the African slave trade, Charleston harbor shipped an estimated 30,000 to 50,000 Indians to the Caribbean "sugar islands" to work in the cane fields.

In those days Carolina exported more Indian slaves than it imported African slaves. But over time, owners came to prefer the African slave. Male Indians were "hard-wired" to be hunter-warriors, not farmhands. And when compared to Africans, escaped Native Americans could more easily fade into their familiar wilderness.

Many Southeastern tribes chose to embrace the white culture and lifestyle. For a minority of the Cherokee, this emulation extended even to the ownership of slaves. Cherokee Chief John Ross owned 100 black slaves. Another wealthy Cherokee is reputed to have owned more than 400 black slaves!

Slaves could be of any skin color. In the mid-1700s, a small but sinister Scottish slave cartel abducted the poor youth of Scotland. They were sold in South Carolina and elsewhere as lowly indentured servants, and faced long odds of regaining freedom.

Slavery in South Carolina also included this quirky fact: During the Revolution, South Carolina legislators sanctioned the practice by American generals of recruiting soldiers by offering each new militiaman "one grown negro slave." This signup bonus increased with rank, so that a lieutenant colonel could expect to receive "three large and one small negro slave."

Only a minority of South Carolinians ever owned slaves, and one in four likely opposed the idea of Confederate secession. Yet upper-class legislators managed to pass harsh and sometimes curious laws meant to preserve the institution of slavery:

One seemingly humane law limited the hours a South Carolina slave must work. But note: in this region where black slaves outnumbered free white citizens, lawmakers always feared a slave rebellion. The above law was merely intended to stave off rebellion by requiring masters to work slaves no more than 15 hours per day, or 105 hours per week!

They Stole Sitting Bull's Bones!

Sitting Bull was born and died in present-day South Dakota. But he was initially buried across the border at Fort Yates, N. D.

His death is attributed to the 1890 Ghost Dance craze, which swept through Lakota reservations. The mystic Wovoka founded this religion, which promoted the idea that believers wearing "ghost shirts" were immune to the cavalry's bullets. Authorities feared the now-elderly Sitting Bull might encourage young ghost dancers. As a precaution, he was to be arrested. Hungry for headlines, Buffalo Bill arrived to help apprehend his old friend.

However, it was determined that Indian police could best secure Sitting Bull's peaceful arrest. On the morning of his arrest, the chief's specially trained horse (a gift from Buffalo Bill's Wild West Show) was brought out as transportation to jail.

At the last minute, Sitting Bull's followers resisted. The old warrior and several others lost their lives in a confusing hail of bullets. To amazed onlookers, the chief's horse responded to gunfire as though it was back in the Wild West Show, commencing a series of tricks! Indians on both sides interpreted the scene as Sitting Bull's soul jumping from his fallen body into that of his "possessed" horse. The tragedy that morning sparked a series of events that led directly to the Wounded Knee Massacre.

For decades, Sitting Bull's remains laid forgotten in that untended North Dakota graveyard. In 1953, a group of historically motivated individuals,

led by Sitting Bull's nephew Clarence Grey Eagle, sought to have the great Lakota leader's remains brought back to South Dakota.

Sitting Bull's surviving relatives agreed with the plan. But negotiations between the governors of North Dakota and South Dakota and other officials repeatedly broke down. Both states wanted Sitting Bull's grave.

On April 8, 1953, Grey Eagle and friends took matters into their own hands. In a dramatic midnight raid on the North Dakota graveyard that involved several vehicles, a backhoe and a light aircraft, Sitting Bull's bones were secretly dug up.

The remains were soon back in South Dakota. To assure that North Dakotans wouldn't steal the bones back, they were encased in a concrete block weighing 20 tons. Then as now, many North Dakotans maintained that the raiding party dug up the wrong grave. The bizarre story received national and international news coverage.

In fact neither state may have the bones. The following unverified story was told to the author in 1979 by the elderly daughter of an army private assigned to bury Sitting Bull. By her account, the ground in North Dakota in January was frozen solid. So the soldiers did the next best thing: They chopped a hole in the nearby frozen Missouri River, and gave the great chief the prairie version of a burial at sea.

SOUTH DAKOTA

Fabled "Lost Sea" Is Found

For many generations a legend persisted of a "Lost Sea" under eastern Tennessee. In 1905, one small boy proved the legend was at least partly true. The so-called Lost Sea lies 300 feet underground where today boats cruise its clear waters. Though more of a lake than a sea, the Lost Sea's actual size is unknown because the main cave connects to larger and deeper water-filled caverns. To date, divers have mapped thirteen acres.

Cherokee Indians performed ceremonies in the upper cavern "Council Room", and early settlers used the cool grotto as a "refrigerator" for vegetables. Even then there were rumors of further chambers leading to a large underground lake. Rumor became fact in 1905 when 13-year-old Ben Sands wiggled through a tiny, muddy opening and found himself in a huge room half-filled with water.

So large was the room that Ben's lantern light was swallowed by the darkness long before reaching the far wall. He threw mud balls as far as he could into the blackness, hearing nothing but distant splashes. When interviewed years later, Sands said, "I knew at that moment I had discovered another world deep within the earth."

For years, Lost Sea reigned as the largest known underground body of water, and was duly listed in the *Guinness Book of Records.* That was before spelunkers recently discovered an underground lake in Africa that is ½ acre larger, relegating Lost Sea to second place.

The clear 70-foot-deep waters of Lost Sea support a unique race of Rainbow Trout. Due to total darkness, these fish become both blind and nearly white. The trout were stocked as part of a project to determine the true size of the lake: Tagged and released to swim where no diver could go, it was hoped they would turn up in a distant pool inside or outside the known cave system. Though this experiment was not successful, the trout have thrived in the cool waters.

Lost Sea and its connecting caverns have a rich history. During Prohibition the cave concealed moonshiners who brewed various illegal beverages. Later, legal libations were served by a local entrepreneur in a dancehall he dubbed the "Cavern Tavern." In those days patrons claimed the cave's air pressure allowed them to drink alcohol without feeling the effects — that is, until those same partiers climbed to the surface, where some stumbled and others passed out.

During the Civil War, the Confederate Army mined the cave for saltpeter, a key element in the manufacture of gunpowder. A diary of the period tells of a Union spy who penetrated the guarded cave and nearly succeeded in blowing up the mining operation. According the diary, he was captured and then executed near the cave entrance.

What is saltpeter? The answer can be traced to a time when the cave was home to thousands of bats. Bats excrete bat guano, which rebel soldiers gathered for its potassium nitrate, or saltpeter, to be shipped to munitions plants. "So basically the Civil War was fought with bat poop," quipped one local wag!

TENNESSEE

True Tale Tops Sleepy Hollow Legend

Few American urban legends are based in fact. However, one such factual tale is of El Muerto, the headless horseman of Texas.

South Texas in the 1800s was a lawless place. Making matters worse, the U.S. claimed the Rio Grande as the border, while Mexico insisted the more northerly Nueces River was the boundary. This left a huge tract of land between the rivers in legal limbo. This godforsaken "No Man's Land" became a haven for cattle and horse thieves. In one year alone, 30,000 head of livestock were lost to banditos.

The most notorious bandito was known simply as Vidal. Showing his true colors in 1836 when he first served as a lieutenant in Santa Ana's army, Vidal defected to the Texan side. By 1850, he was the uncontested leader of South Texas livestock rustlers.

But when Vidal and his men stole a string of horses near the headwaters of the San Antonio River, he unknowingly nabbed several steeds belonging to feared Texas Ranger Creed Taylor. Before long, Taylor and fellow Texas Ranger William "Big Foot" Wallace were in hot pursuit of Vidal and his gang.

Horse theft was then a capital offense. So when Taylor and Big Foot caught up with the thieves, they dispensed "frontier justice" by killing all, including Vidal.

For years the Rangers had tried to send a "message" that crime doesn't pay by stringing up convicts to shrivel and rot in the Texas sun — or chopping them to pieces. Because these grizzly deterrents hadn't worked, Wallace and Taylor decided to add a twist: Big Foot Wallace beheaded Vidal, and then lashed the body to the high Mexican saddle on the back of a wild mustang. Big Foot's finishing touch was to loosely attach Vidal's severed head, and then turn the horse loose to wander the Texas Hill Country.

Before long, stories began to circulate of the dark horse with its fearsome rider. More than one cowboy attempted long-range shots at the skittish horse and bizarre rider, always without effect. Thus grew the real-life legend of El Muerto, the headless one.

Finally, a posse of ranchers captured the dark mustang at a water hole south of Alice, Texas. Still strapped to its back was the now mummified body of Vidal, riddled with bullet holes and broken arrows. In the year *after* Vidal's body was laid to rest, soldiers at Fort Inge (present-day Uvalde) reported multiple sightings of a headless horseman.

Folk tales from Ireland, Germany and elsewhere mention headless horsemen. America has Washington Irving's "The Legend of Sleepy Hollow." More recently a headless equestrian rode briefly through the pages of the Harry Potter series. But none can match El Muerto, history's only real headless horseman.

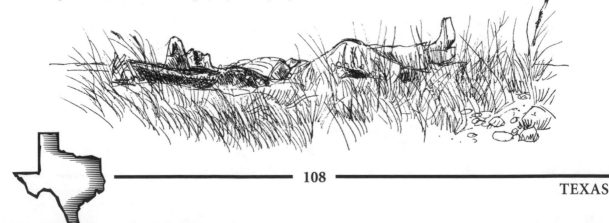

America's Weird and Wacky Borders

You've got to love America's occasionally loony boundaries! A case in point is Minnesota's Northwest Angle. Accessible solely by air or by crossing Canada's Lake of the Woods, this is the only part of America, excluding Alaska, that is north of the famed 49th parallel. Or take Point Roberts, a similarly separated enclave of Washington State. (Read more about Point Roberts on page 149.)

The storied Arizona Strip, that portion of Arizona north of the Grand Canyon, was originally part of Utah Territory. It made practical sense to put the border on this natural divide. But when the Missouri Compromise allowed slavery south of latitude 36 degrees 30 minutes, Congress eventually voted to assign the Strip to Arizona Territory (where slave ownership was technically legal). Today the Arizona Strip is a mostly empty landscape developed in part by polygamous religious sects. To visit their county seat, residents of the Strip must travel through southern Utah, the tip of Nevada, a portion of California, and then back into Arizona. Many attempts have been made to return the Strip and its predominately Mormon residents to Utah, but none has succeeded.

Further west is a highly inprobable 18-mile slice of sunny California that is actually *NORTH* of Canada. Your atlas will clearly show a thin point of sand dunes, Point Pelee, jutting deep into Lake Ontario. In fact, this southernmost part of Canada is south of the ocean beaches of Smith River, Calif.

Weird boundaries also include this unexpected zigzag of one American time zone: When it is high noon in Pensacola, Florida, it is also high noon at historic Fort Union on the North Dakota-Montana border! Counterintuitively, both locations are in the Central time zone.

Utah shares a point of mathematical perfection known as Four Corners, the place where the Beehive State meets at right angles with Colorado, Arizona and New Mexico. It is the only point in the United States where four states meet.

In 1949, the governor of Utah met his counterparts from Colorado, Arizona and New Mexico for a business lunch at a table set up precisely over the Four Corners. Each governor sat in his own state, passing food around the table from one state to another.

Four Corners was originally declared by Congress to be 37° north, 109° west, but an early surveyor made a mistake when he marked the location. The U.S. Supreme Court later ruled that the current location had become so standard that it should be officially recognized as the actual boundary between the four states. Thus, some say the current monument, administered by the Navajo Nation and featuring a platform allowing tourists to stand in four states at once, is misplaced. It should be a long stone's throw to the northeast.

There would be no Four Corners at all, if it wasn't for another surveyor's accommodation on the Utah–Colorado line. The border between the two states may appear straight, in which case you don't have a big enough map. Southeast of La Sal, Utah, is a 1.5-mile adjustment to the border. Without this corrective jog in the boundary line, there could be no Four Corners further south!

First Railroad Across America — Or Was It?

12:45 p.m., May 10, 1869. History tells us this is the exact moment when a "Golden Spike" was struck to complete the first railroad across North America. The old photo of the Union Pacific and Central Pacific locomotives meeting at Promontory Point, Utah, is etched in our collective memory. But this is only part of a larger truth.

The event at Promontory Point was well promoted. That final spike was wired to a telegraph pole, announcing each ceremonial blow of the hammer to a waiting world, and triggering cannon blasts and celebrations from San Francisco to New York City.

This supposed first continuous ribbon of rail between the Atlantic and Pacific actually was interrupted by river crossings, most notably over the Missouri River at Omaha. Here the first transcontinental trains had to be broken up into car lengths, with engine and cars ferried one by one across the wide Missouri.

Eight months after the Golden Spike ceremony, in January 1870, an ice bridge was completed over the frozen Missouri at Omaha. This continuous band of rails truly connected the oceans, but only temporarily! Within two months the spring thaw made the nearly 1/3rd mile ice bridge too dangerous.

Thanks to the great iron bridge over the Missouri at Kansas City, the Kansas Pacific's plan to unite Kansas City and Denver by rail also promised to create the first legitimate and continuous transcontinental rail connection.

The Union Pacific wouldn't complete a Missouri River bridge at Omaha until 1872.

Kansas Pacific crews worked west from Missouri and east from Denver. It was predicted that the Kansas Pacific rails would meet at Comanche Crossing, a lonely spot on the high prairie just east of Strasburg, Colo. Here Old Glory was run up a makeshift flagpole, and the two crews raced to be first to the flag.

And so at Comanche Crossing, tracklayers met at the nearly forgotten time and date of 3 p.m., Aug. 15, 1870, to forge a true transcontinental railroad. This was 14 months after Utah's "Golden Spike" event. In Colorado there was no golden spike, and little ceremony, though an estimated 1,000 people witnessed the meeting of the rails. Now Denver was linked to both oceans.

In an interesting footnote of the rush to Promontory Point, elite tracklayers of the Central Pacific laid 10 miles and 56 feet of rail in a single day. This was a world track laying record. Union Pacific tracklayers wanted to challenge the record, but lacked a sufficient stockpile of rails. When the Kansas Pacific was nearing completion, some of these same disappointed Union Pacific workers transferred to Colorado for a second chance at the record. They joined other workers on that historic Ides of August to lay 10 miles plus 1,320 feet of rail to claim a new world record.

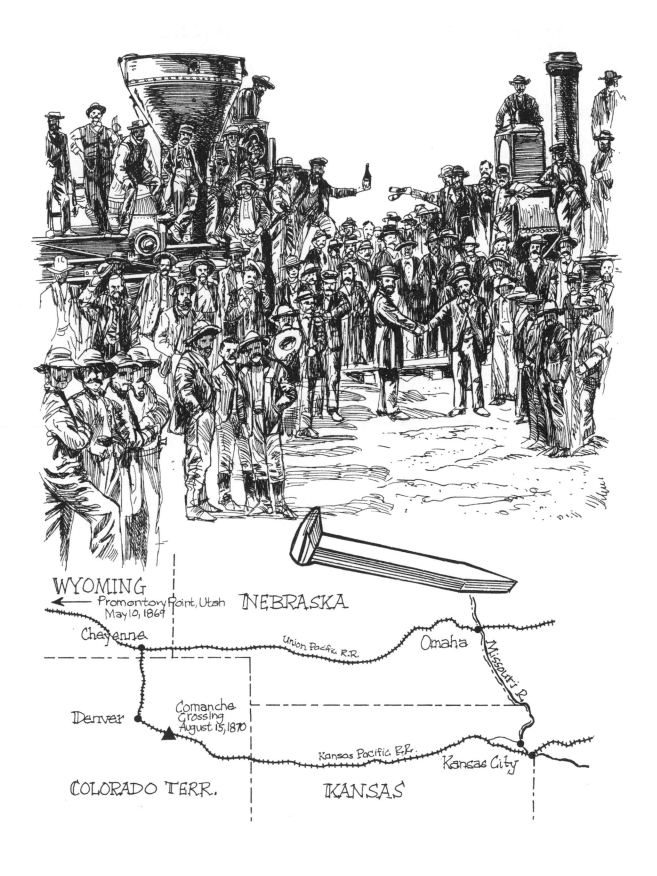

WYOMING
← Promontory Point, Utah
May 10, 1869

NEBRASKA

Cheyenne

Union Pacific R.R.

Omaha

Missouri R.

Denver

Comanche
Crossing
August 15, 1870

Kansas Pacific R.R.

Kansas City

COLORADO TERR.

KANSAS

Green Mountain Boys Get Last Laugh

His larger-than-life statue stands under the Capitol dome, shoulder to shoulder with America's Founding Fathers. Yet some claim Ethan Allen's first allegiance was to the state he created, even if that meant his state must join British Canada — or the fledging United States — or remain forever separate as the Republic of Vermont.

Never one of the original 13 colonies, Ethan Allen's Vermont was claimed and heavily taxed by both New York and New Hampshire. This jeopardized Allen's vast holdings, but he found a way to legitimize his property deeds by the pen *and* the sword.

Following America's Declaration of Independence, Vermonters gathered at a tavern in Windsor to make a similar declaration. The resulting Constitution of the Republic of Vermont went far beyond the U.S. Constitution in guaranteeing personal freedoms. It was the first constitution in the New World to prohibit slavery, guarantee male voting rights regardless of race, religon or property ownership, and promise a free education to both genders.

For 14 years, the nascent Republic of Vermont issued currency, operated a postal system, saluted a national flag and maintained a standing army famously known as the Green Mountain Boys. Early in the American Revolution, Col. Allen and his Green Mountain Boys capturing Fort Ticonderoga from the British. The cannon and powder Allen commandeered were later used by George Washington to drive the British out of Boston.

Military valor earned a certain status for Allen and Vermont, yet Vermont's petition to join the new union of states was repeatedly blocked by New Yorkers. "Vermont is, after all, part of New York," proclaimed New York Governor George Clinton, who later put a bounty on Ethan Allen's head.

Frustrated, Allen began secret negotiations with the British to preserve Vermont sovereignty, or alternately to gain admission to British Canada. Was this a ploy to coax Congress into annexing Vermont? Allen's negotiations would bring accusations of treason.

Many years later, Vermont joined the United States as the 14th state, but only after powerful New York dropped its earlier objections. The reason? New Yorkers determined that when the next Congress convened, abolitionist Vermont would counterbalance the anticipated admission of Kentucky, a slave state.

Sadly, Ethan Allen died before Vermont's admission to the Union. Historians agree: Allen was rather calculating in his defense of Vermont and his own interests. But those who say he was a mere fair weather patriot might consider this story, often told by Abraham Lincoln:

During a post-war visit to England, Allen's hosts entertained him cordially. But they also repeatedly ridiculed Americans, whom they still considered wayward colonists. To further annoy Allen, his hosts hung a portrait of Washington on the outhouse wall. When teasingly asked his thoughts on the picture's placement, Ethan Allen calmly retorted, "It is most appropriately hung. There is nothing that will make an Englishman shit so quick as the sight of General Washington."

Ethan Allen

Secrets of George Washington's Death Revealed

We know the date and strange circumstances of the death of Virginia's George Washington. Details of his birth are less certain. Calendars typically list his birthday as Feb. 22, 1732. Yet in some texts his birthday is Feb. 11, 1731. Impossible as it seems, both dates are perfectly correct. Here's why:

In colonial times, the primitive Julian calendar was still used. According to this calendar New Year's Day is March 25. Known as Lady Day, it marked the conception of Jesus at the Annunciation, which in turn established the much-debated date for Christmas precisely nine months later.

In 1752, Britain and its colonies adopted the modern Gregorian calendar. To "synchronize" new and old calendars, the British skipped 11 days in an exercise similar to daylight saving time adjustments. Many colonial Americans then living also adjusted their birth date, so their next birthday would be 365 days after their last. George Washington was the most prominent person to have done so. In 1753 and afterward he reckoned his birth date as Feb. 22, 1732, not Feb. 11, 1731 as it had been on the old calendar.

Though never wounded in battle, Washington had many close calls. At the Battle of the Wilderness, he had two horses shot from under him, and his hat was shot off! After the battle, close examination revealed four bullet holes in his uniform.

An imposing 6 feet 2 inches tall, and of strong physique, Washington was seen by contemporaries as a good candidate to live at least four-score years (80). It was not to be:

On Dec. 12, 1799, Washington spent a cold, rainy day on horseback overseeing his beloved Mount Vernon estate. The ex-president thereafter developed what was probably only a bad cold, or perhaps bronchitis. At dawn on Dec. 14, Washington called on his aides to perform the then fashionable medical quackery of bloodletting. At 10 a.m., the general's old army surgeon James Craik arrived, and bled him again. An hour later yet another physician came, and Washington was bled again. At 3 p.m. other doctors arrived, and as part of their treatment they opened the great statesman's veins a fourth time. A total of 80 ounces of blood were removed in 12 hours, amounting to nearly 35 percent of the blood in the ex-president's body.

Thus died the Father of America — a man who fought nearly 100 battles without ever being wounded was bled to death by his own doctors. George Washington was 67.

The day after the apparent death of Washington, eminent physician William Thornton arrived at Mount Vernon. Thornton hoped that Washington was in a suspended state, from which he could be reanimated and then treated. Washington's body had been packed in ice after his death.

Thornton proposed thawing the body gradually — first in cool water and then with warm blankets and rubbing of the skin, with a subsequent tracheotomy, artificial respiration at the tracheotomy site and a transfusion of lamb's blood.

Martha Washington firmly vetoed Thornton's plans for a "resurrection." Interestingly, George Washington had once revived a slave presumed to be dead. Dr. Thornton was likely aware of this story.

Missing! — Planet's Biggest Waterfall

When driving through Dry Falls, Wash., be sure to get out of the car and look up at what's left of history's mightiest waterfall. Though today not a drop of water trickles over the 400-foot precipice, ages ago this was the BIG ONE — ten times bigger than Niagara Falls.

Such a falls demanded the world's largest source of flowing water — nothing less than a flood of biblical proportions would suffice. But where would such a massive amount of water come from here in eastern Washington's high, dry desert?

The scientific community struggles to verify a deluge matching the Genesis flood. But growing evidence points to a North American version of Noah's torrent: The Lake Missoula Flood is the largest documented flood in earth history.

It all started during the last Ice Age. As glaciers moved south, one ice sheet plugged the the Columbia River, blocking water that drained out of Montana. The resulting Lake Missoula covered much of western Montana, empounding enough water to fill modern-day Lake Ontario.

Then about 14,500 years ago, the ice dam collapsed to release an "inland tsunami" that raced through Washington. Lake Missoula emptied in less than 48 hours. Lands as far away as northwest Oregon flooded. Present-day Portland was inundated by 400 vertical feet of water.

This process of ice-damming of the river, a refilling of Lake Missoula, and subsequent cataclysmic flooding, repeated many times during the last Ice Age.

Giant floods caused one giant waterfall where these torrents of water poured off Washington's central plateau. As with most waterfalls, the undercutting action of water caused the great falls to retreat over the decades. At one location geologists estimate the falls was nearly 1,000 feet tall and four miles across.

Anthropologists believe Asians probably entered the Americas during this most recent glacial epoch, 13,000-14,000 years ago. Thus, we have an intriguing possibility: Could the last of these great flood/waterfall episodes have been witnessed by a stunned band of early Americans?

Imagine for a moment the first fur-clad Paleo-Indians as they round the corner of a canyon, to confront this largest of all waterfalls. Though bone dry today, the peak flow of Dry Falls would have been ten times greater than all the world's rivers combined! The ground-shaking sound, sight and feel would have been the greatest spectacle ever witnessed.

Heavenly Isle Hides Conspirators

Some have called this West Virginia island the most beautiful in the New World. The paradise isle, a favorite of Indian chiefs, was also visited by King Charles X of France, Johnny Appleseed, Henry Clay and Walt Whitman. It was named for Harman Blennerhassett, the Irish aristocrat forced from his castle and homeland because of the sin of wedding his niece.

The Blennerhassetts found their fresh start on the island, where they built a famed mansion overlooking the Ohio River. Here in 1805, Harman received a visit from former Vice President Aaron Burr. Thus began Blennerhassett Island's role as headquarters for a scheme to establish a new nation carved from the Louisiana Purchase, or Spanish Texas.

Aaron Burr was the most controversial man of his era:

- A revolutionary war hero, Burr ran for president against Thomas Jefferson in 1800. The titans each gained 37 electoral votes.
- This tie election was ultimately decided by Congress. But it took 36 ballots before Jefferson was declared president. As was the custom of the day, the losing presidential candidate assumed the vice presidency.
- While vice president, Burr killed his nemesis, Secretary of Treasury Alexander Hamilton, in America's most notable pistol duel.

Next for Burr was the grand conspiracy, with Blennerhasset Island at its axis. Many historians believe Burr planned to use Harman Blennerhasset's fortune to finance an independent nation in the West, with New Orleans as its capital and Burr as emperor.

When President Jefferson learned of the conspiracy, he ordered both men imprisoned for treason. The courts of the day were unable to secure a conviction in either case. But the publicity ruined Blennerhasset, and he never returned to his island paradise.

Blennerhassett Island was the northwest frontier of Virginia at a time when Virginia was our biggest state (roughly the size of Oklahoma). Decades later a minority of Western Virginians would use the Civil War as an excuse to create a brand new state.

The frontiersmen of Virginia's rugged Western districts had always resented domination by the rich planters of the Eastern counties. So when Virginia seceded, certain interests in the West declared a new state called Kanawha. They soon changed the name to West Virginia, held a highly questionable statehood referendum, and petitioned Washington D.C. for admission to the Union.

Lincoln's cabinet was deeply divided. After all, the U.S. Constitution was clear: "No new States shall be formed or erected within the Jurisdiction of any other State … without the Consent of the Legislature of the State concerned." Obviously, the rebel Virginia legislature wasn't about to give consent.

Today's constitutional scholars agree that the creation of our 35th state, West Virginia, was of questionable legality. Still, it's worth viewing the 35-star spangled banner flying from the Capitol during the Civil War. That 35th star was West Virginia. But as Lincoln often pointed out, his flag also stubbornly bore a star for Virginia and every other Confederate state.

Harman Blennerhassett   Aaron Burr

Blennerhassett Island

Flying Boulders Flatten Bedrooms

It may be true that lightning rarely strikes the same place twice. But at 440 North Shore Drive in Fountain City, Wis., boulders seemingly tumble from the sky and plunge through roofs … not once, but twice in the same century!

On April 24, 1995, a 55-ton boulder bounced nearly 500 feet down a cliff above the Mississippi River, crashing through the roof and landing in the master bedroom of Maxine and Dwight Anderson's home. At the moment of impact, Maxine had just exited the bedroom, where she was ironically taking snapshots of a recently completed remodeling.

The shaken Andersons moved out immediately, returning only long enough to pack their belongings. But real estate agent John Burt saw dollar signs in the severely damaged house. He promptly bought it — not to live in, but to open as a tourist attraction.

The naming of the "Rock in the House" was intended to poke gentle fun at another well-known Wisconsin attraction: Spring Green's architecture gem the "House on the Rock." But unlike just about every other tourist stop, Rock in the House is run strictly on the honor system. Simply walk in the front door and a series of hand-written notes requests a $1 admission. Signs then direct you to another door, behind which lies the great brooding boulder, still wedged sideways between the walls of the master bedroom.

Even after finishing the tour, you might not know the property's complete and rather bizarre story. The garage out back is the site of a home once belonging to the retired Mr. and Mrs. Dubler. In 1901, an eerily similar but more tragic event unfolded: This time the boulder careened down the cliff in the dark of night and landed squarely on the bed of the slumbering couple. Mrs. Dubler was instantly crushed to death. Her blind husband, sleeping at her side, was plunged into the cellar, where rescuers found him uninjured except for a small bump on his forehead!

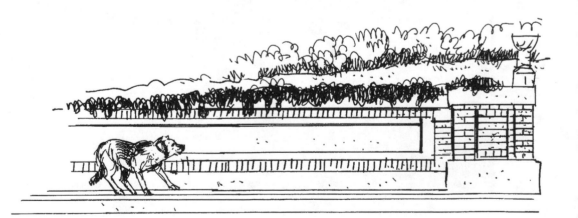

Gold Rumor Triggers Stampede

If we could hear again the sounds of the gold rush to the Black Hills, one of those sounds would be the rumble of a stampede. The biggest Black Hills stampedes weren't caused by cattle or thundering buffalo, but by the prospectors themselves!

Stampedes to new diggings were fairly common in the last great gold rush of the Old West, the Black Hills gold rush. Prospectors were always eager to try their luck elsewhere, and rumors of a big strike over the next hill could stampede miners in a new direction.

There were stampedes to Bear Gulch, to False Bottom Creek, and to the nearby Bear Lodge Mountains of Wyoming. But strangest of all was the ill-fated Wolf Mountains Stampede.

This stampede started on the streets of Deadwood in November, 1876. Winter was coming, and hay was scarce, which meant lean times for livery stables that bought and sold horses. The one exception was Red Clark's stables, for Clark was busy buying up horses at bottom dollar.

It is now believed that Clark also arranged for an accomplice to circulate false rumors of a fabulous gold strike in the Wolf Mountains. Rumor spread like wildfire, and the Wolf Mountains Stampede was on. Saddle horses were suddenly in great demand, and stable owners like Red Clark wore big smiles.

Historian Watson Parker estimates that 1,500 prospectors used countless horses in a mad dash to the Wolf Mountains. Incredible as it sounds, few who joined the rush knew the exact location of the Wolf Mountains. Popular opinion held that the mountains must be in the vicinity of the distant Bighorn Range of present-day Wyoming. An alleged "bald peak" was said to mark the new diggings, but neither peak nor gold was ever found.

The Wolf Mountains Stampede may have been the greatest deception in Black Hills history – perpetrated for profit on the sale of horses. In the long winter that followed, many hoaxed and haggard stampeders filtered back to Deadwood. Some returned with frozen toes or fingers.

Some never returned.

When Doomsday Came Calling in Your State

Thus far, the United States has avoided a catastrophic accident involving nuclear weapons. Basic safeguards have thwarted most accidental detonations. Luck, too, has played a role. The following sample of unclassified accidents proves no region of the country is unaffected. The full list is presumed to be classified:

Fairbanks, **Alaska**, February 1950: In the world's first nuclear weapons accident, a B-36 bomber en route from Eielson Air Force Base (AFB) to Carswell Air Force Base (AFB), Texas, encountered bad weather and icing, forcing the crew to jettison a nuclear weapon into the Pacific Ocean. All 16 crew members and one passenger parachuted to safety.

Lebanon, **Ohio**, July 1950: A B-50 bomber carrying a nuclear weapon crashed near here on a training run originating in El Paso, Texas. The weapon's non-nuclear high explosives detonated on impact, creating a 25-foot-deep crater.

Fairfield, **California**, August 1950: A B-29 bomber from Suison Air Force Base, carrying a nuclear warhead without its fissile core, crashed and burned near a trailer park occupied by 200 families.

Tampa, **Florida**, March 1956: A B-47 bomber transporting two nuclear weapons cores in their carrying cases departed Tampa's MacDill Air Force Base. The aircraft failed to contact a tanker over the Mediterranean Sea for a scheduled in-flight refueling. Despite an extensive search, no trace of the aircraft, nuclear cores, or crew were ever found.

Delaware and New Jersey, July 1957: A C-124 aircraft transporting three nuclear weapons lost power in two engines. The crew was forced to jettison the weapons somewhere east of Rehoboth Beach, Delaware and Cape May/Windwood, New Jersey, where the bombs presumably still lie on the ocean floor.

Homestead Air Force Base, **Florida**, October 1957: A B-47 bomber carrying a nuclear weapon and a separate fissile core crashed shortly after takeoff. The bomb, weapons core and carrying case were recovered intact.

Savannah, **Georgia**, February 1958: A nuclear weapon without fissile core was lost following a mid-air collision near Savannah. Extensive searches failed to locate the weapon, though it is believed to be underwater near the mouth of Savannah River off the Tybee Island beach.

Florence, **South Carolina**, March 1958: A B-47E bomber accidentally dropped an unarmed nuclear weapon into the garden of Walter Gregg. The bomb's conventional explosives created a crater 70 feet wide, destroying Gregg's house and slightly injuring him and five family members. Following the accident, Air Force crews were ordered to "lock in" all nuclear bombs. This reduced the risk of accidental drops, but ironically increased the risk to crew members during a plane crash.

Whidbey Island, **Washington**, September 1959: A U.S. Navy P5M Marlin aircraft carrying an unarmed nuclear depth charge crashed into Puget Sound near Whidbey Island. The weapon was never recovered.

Trenton, **New Jersey,** June 1960: An atomic air defense missile being stored at McGuire Air Force Base in a ready state (permitting its launch in two minutes) was destroyed when a high-pressure helium tank exploded. Although

When Doomsday Came Calling in Your State

a *New York Times* article described it as a near nuclear disaster, the safety devices acted properly and prevented the weapon's detonation.

Monticello, **Utah,** January 1961: A B-52 bomber carrying one nuclear weapon exploded in midair near here. It was on a training mission from Biggs Air Force Base in **Texas** to Bismarck, North Dakota.

Goldsboro, **North Carolina**, January 1961: A B-52 bomber on airborne alert carrying two nuclear weapons broke apart in midair. One weapon's parachute malfunctioned, and the weapon broke apart on impact. According to military analyst Daniel Ellsburg, "five of the

Continued

Dale Crawford

When Doomsday Came Calling in Your State

six safety devices had failed." Nuclear physicist Ralph Lapp confirmed this, saying "… only a single switch … had prevented the nuclear bomb from detonating." Despite an extensive search of surrounding farmland, the weapons-grade uranium core was never recovered, prompting the Air Force to purchase an easement requiring permission before any digging or construction in the area.

Yuba City, **California**, March 1961: A B-52 bomber carrying two nuclear weapons crashed. Cause of the crash: the plane ran out of fuel. This happened when the cabin pressurization system failed, forcing the plane to descend to 10,000 feet and thus increasing the plane's fuel consumption.

Camp Douglas, **Wisconsin**, October 1962: During the height of the Cuban missile crisis, an alarm signaled that a nuclear war with the Soviet Union was commencing. Pilots ran to their nuclear-armed aircraft at Volk Field Air National Guard Base, southwest of Tomah, and were ready to take off when the false alarm was detected.

Peru, **Indiana**, December 1964: A B-58 bomber slid off a runway at Grissom Air Force Base. The resulting fire consumed portions of five onboard nuclear weapons, resulting in limited radioactive contamination of the area.

Denver, **Colorado**, May 1969: A plutonium fire broke out at Rocky Flats Weapons Plant. Several of the buildings were so badly contaminated they were dismantled.

Pauling, **New York**, December 1972: A major fire and two explosions at a plutonium fabrication plant resulted in the plant's permanent shutdown.

Erwin, **Tennessee**, August 1979: Enriched uranium was accidentally released from a top-secret nuclear fuel plant. Approximately 1,000 people received slight radiation contamination.

Livermore, **California**, January 1980: A magnitude 5.5 earthquake at Lawrence Livermore National Laboratory caused a tritium radiation leak.

Damascus, **Arkansas**, September 1980: Fuel vapors from a Titan II intercontinental ballistic missile exploded in the missile's silo, blowing off the silo's 740-ton door of reinforced concrete and steel, and catapulting the missile's nuclear warhead 600 feet. The accident occurred when a repairman dropped a wrench socket that struck the missile, causing a leak in its pressurized fuel tank.

Grand Forks, **North Dakota**, September 1980: A B-52 bomber carrying nuclear short-range attack missiles caught fire while on the ground during an alert exercise. Strong prairie winds blew from a fortuitous direction to help firefighters keep the fire away from the missiles.

Cheyenne, **Wyoming**, January 1984: A recorded message at Warren Air Force Base stated that a Minuteman III intercontinental ballistic missile was about to launch from its silo due to a computer error. To prevent launch, an armored car was parked on top of the silo.

Thumbing Through America's Weird Past

A few years after Columbus' epic voyages, Italian explorer Giovanni da Verrazzano cruised America's East Coast. He was impressed by a wide bay he called Santa Margarita, known today as New York Harbor. Further north he encountered feisty natives who bared their buttocks at sailors and teasingly lowered trade goods onto the rocks where the breakers were most violent. To Verrazzano it was the "Land of Bad People." Today we call it **Maine**.

In Vermont, nearly 15,000 residents speak French as their first language. Like other states bordering Quebec, Vermont's current jobs and earlier ill-defined borders have attracted French Canadians wishing to flee British influence. There's a large enough French-speaking population in Winooski, Vermont that the local cable TV system is obligated to carry two French stations out of Montreal.

The slogan on **New Hampshire** license plates is "Live Free or Die." Ironically, these license plates are manufactured by prisoners at the state prison in Concord.

It was surely North America's smallest independent country, with just 301 souls populating a territory barely ten miles wide by 25 miles long. The Republic of Indian Stream declared independence on July 9, 1832. The establishment of Indian Stream as an independent nation was the result of ill-defined boundaries between the United States and British Canada written into the Treaty of Paris after the Revolutionary War.

For several decades the region was a sort of No Mans Land. When both Canada and the United States began sending tax collectors into the disputed region, frustrated locals declared independence as a last resort. Soon the little nation had it's own bicameral legislature, constitution, court system, postage stamps, and even a 41-man militia.

Nearly four years passed before Britian relinquished its claim to the parcel, but only after the tiny republic's Congress voted in favor of annexation by the United States. Today the former Indian Stream Republic is extreme northern **New Hampshire**.

The 60-story John Hancock Tower in **Boston** is haunted by the strangest problem in skyscraper annals: Its huge windows — 4- x 11-foot panes of glass — pop out unexpectedly and shatter on the street below. The building was less than a month old when, in 1972, windows began popping out for no apparent reason. To remedy the situation, the building's owners replaced all 10,334 windows with 400-pound sections of half-inch tempered glass. The windows kept popping out. Today the mystery remains unsolved, and windows occasionally still break free. To protect pedestrians, John Hancock Tower employs two full-time guard whose only task is to spot a cracked pane before it tumbles to the sidewalk.

On a winter day in 1919, an enormous vat of molasses exploded at a factory in **Boston's** North End. The 50-foot-tall vat spilled 2.5 million gallons of molasses in a sticky "tidal wave" through the streets. The Boston Molasses Massacre killed 21 people and injured another 150. A nearby fire station was blown off its foundation.

Wrote one stunned onlooker, "Molasses, waist deep, covered the street and swirled and bubbled about … Here and there struggled a form — whether it was animal or human being was impossible to tell … Horses died like so many flies on sticky fly-paper." Boston Harbor appeared brown with molasses for six months. To this day, some North Enders will tell you that on hot summer afternoons it's possible to smell the molasses that thoroughly soaked their neighborhood.

John Kennedy was awarded a Pulitzer Prize in 1957 for *Profiles in Courage*, a book he probably didn't write. It's believed Kennedy's ghostwriter for the book was Theodore Sorensen, one of his speech writers.

Four U.S. states don't consider themselves states at all — **Massachusetts**, Pennsylvania, Virginia and Kentucky are actually commonwealths, even though the federal government refuses to acknowledge any distinction between states and commonwealths. Early in its history, **Rhode Island** was sometimes referred to as a commonwealth. Incidentally, our smallest state has the longest *official* state name: "The State of Rhode Island and Providence Plantations."

The original 13 colonies and later the various states often minted or attempted to mint their own currency. Later came the famous federally produced silver dollar, which was minted to contain precisely one dollar's worth of silver. It circulated interchangeably with the Spanish silver dollar throughout post-revolutionary America. Later the various Confederate States were responsible for minting their own currency. But the strangest coin ever minted was by a **Connecticut** copper mine owner in 1737. Although people typically treated his copper coin as if it was worth three-pence, the legend on the coin read, "Value me as you please."

New York's revolution-era firebrand Thomas Paine proposed that the closing phrase "…so help me God" found in the presidential oath be made optional. It is indeed optional, but has been spoken by many presidents. Only a minority of historians believe Washington uttered the phrase at his inauguration. Lincoln omitted the phrase at his first presidential oath, but included it as he entered his second term.

Horace Greeley, early editor of the *New York Tribune*, was approached by a stranger who expressed his disapproval of the newspaper: "I used to read that sheet, but now I subscribe to a decent paper. I feed the *Tribune* to my goat." Greeley sized up the man, and said, "Is that so? Well sir, you keep reading your other paper and feeding your goat the *Tribune* and one day your goat will know more than you do."

Future President Grover Cleveland was formerly sheriff of Erie County, New York, where he also filled in as executioner when the usual executioner was unavailable. In this capacity, he killed two men by tightening nooses around their necks and then dropping the trapdoor. This earned our future president his dubious nickname, "the Hangman of Buffalo."

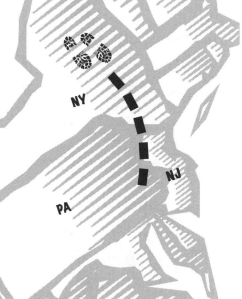

Our Declaration of Independence was issued from **Philadelphia** on July 4, 1776, but wasn't actually signed until August 2. On September 9, the Continental Congress changed the new nation's name from the United Colonies to the United States.

The fabled Underground Railroad was a clandestine network of persons willing to guide escaped slaves to freedom in the "free" states or in Canada. The network could take many forms as evidenced by the case of Samuel Burris, a free black man from Philadelphia. Burris was arrested in Delaware for providing help to an escaping slave. He was found guilty, sentenced to jail, fined, and sold into servitude. The auction came, and he was sold to the highest bidder. As Samuel left with his new owner, he thought he was descending into slavery. But Samuel soon discovered the high bidder was an abolitionist, and he was taken back to Philadelphia …and freedom.

At the revolution-era Battle of Springfield in **New Jersey**, an obscure American hero named Reverend James Caldwell was looking for a way to avenge the killing of his wife by the British a few days earlier. Supplies ran low for the outnumbered colonial forces, including paper needed for wadding for their muskets. Already known as the "Fighting Parson," Caldwell came running out of his Presbyterian church with hymnal books in hand. The pages torn from the hymnals for wadding contained songs by composer Isaac Watts, which explains Caldwell's now famous exhortation to the troops: "Now give 'em Watts, boys. Give 'em Watts!" The British were repulsed, but not before much of the town was burned.

The annual Return Day Pageant in Georgetown, **Delaware** includes this arcane but very American bit of theater. In fact, it's so American that it's *Native* American:

The Pageant features a parade with high school bands, firefighters and little league champs. Then an ox is roasted in the town square, and free sandwiches are provided to all.

But the event that gives Return Day its name dates from 1791, when "returns" were counted in one of the first free elections held in the United States. That's when locals decided it would be wonderful if the winning *and* losing candidates stood side-by-side, and together plunged a ceremonial hatchet into a container of sand. This symbolic "burying of the hatchet" was borrowed from local Indian tradition. For modern Delaware residents, the ceremony is a reminder that the days following an election should be spent healing wounds, and acknowledging that we are, after all, a bipartisan nation.

Thanks to its mountains, ocean beaches, swamps, forests and farmland, **Maryland** was designated by *National Geographic* as the state most representative, in "microcosm," of the greater United States.

Ten American cities claim to once have been the nation's capital — partly because during the Revolutionary War, Americans resorted to a "capital on wheels" to avoid the British Redcoats. One such capital was Annapolis, **Maryland**, the site of what historian Thomas Fleming described as the most important moment in American history.

In Annapolis, a rather timid Congress was congratulating itself on surviving the Revolutionary War. Before this body rose a man with trembling hands and tear-stained cheeks. It was George Washington, soon to deliver a speech as short as it was powerful. In a one-page proclamation, he resigned his commission as commander-in-chief of the Army and retired from public life.

Contemporaries had encouraged Washington to crown himself king, or at least "president for life." Instead, his refusal to seize power ensured democratic civilian rule rather than military rule for the fledgling nation. So profound was the moment that spectators wept openly. When word reached Europe, leaders and commoners alike were awed, for what seemed like the first time in recorded history, "We the People" had trumped "Me."

NJ

MD

DE

District of Columbia Curiosities

While Franklin Pierce was president, he accidentally ran over an old woman with his horse and was arrested. The arresting officer released the President when he discovered who he had in custody. Decades later, President Ulysses S. Grant was arrested for exceeding the speed limit in his horse carriage.

The first U.S. Congress voted to pay George Washington the annual presidental salary of $25,000, about $570,000 in 2009 terms. Washington was already a wealthy man and refused to accept his salary. However, he asked that his living expenses be covered. Theodore Roosevelt spent his entire $50,000 salary on entertaining guests at the White House. John Kennedy donated his salary to charities.

Since the 1970s, many of its residents have supported statehood for the **District of Columbia**. A proposal to seek statehood won the approval of voters in a 1980 election, and the state name "New Columbia" was selected by voters two years later. In 1992, the U.S. House of Representatives passed a measure approving statehood for our federal district, but the Senate refused to consider it.

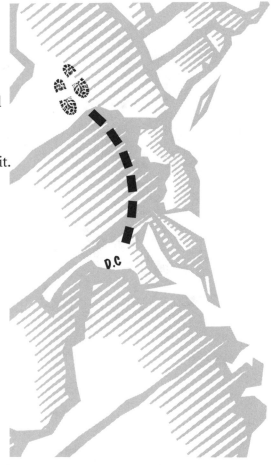

During the War of 1812, British forces invaded Washington and burned the Capitol building, the White House, and other public buildings. Each was rebuilt within five years, but for decades Washington remained a crude, rough town. In 1842, English author Charles Dickens described it as a "monument raised to a deceased project," consisting of "…spacious avenues that begin in nothing and lead nowhere."

During World War One, President Woodrow Wilson instructed that sheep be allowed to graze on the White House lawn. Their wool was shorn and donated to the war effort.

America's 10th president was John Tyler (1841-1845). A lifelong slave owner, Tyler later sided with the Confederate States and served in the Confederate Congress prior to his death in 1862. Because of his allegiance to the Confederacy, Tyler's was the only death in presidential history not to be officially mourned in Washington. Tyler is sometimes considered the only president to die outside the United States, as his place of death, Richmond, Virginia, was part of the Confederate States at the time.

There were probably people who would have wished Tyler dead. To settle theories that Tyler might have been poisoned (most notably by strychnine), his body was exhumed in 1991. With permission of descendants, samples of the remains were analyzed. Some arsenic was found, but in quantities said to be too small to cause harm. This hasn't satisfied some commentators, who found flaws with the testing methods.

The "Father of our Nation" never was a father biologically. George and Martha Washington apparently couldn't conceive children. Some speculate that an early bout with smallpox followed by probable tuberculosis left the first president sterile.

White Sulphur Springs, **West Virginia** has kept a "secret" for 40 years — 800 feet beneath the town's famous Greenbrier Resort is a 112,500-square-foot bunker built in the 1960s to house the members of Congress, plus support staff, in case of a nuclear attack.

When work began on Summersville Dam, the Army Corps of Engineers faced a dilemma. Corps tradition is to name a dam site for the nearest town, which in this case was Gad, West Virginia. After briefly considering the name "Gad Dam," the Corps broke with tradition and named the dam after the next nearest town: Summersville.

Thurmond, **West Virginia** earned a reputation as a rollicking coal town. That reputation was further enhanced by a legendary poker game at the Dunglen Hotel. A rotating cast of card sharks began playing in 1916 and continued non-stop for 14 years. The game ended only when the hotel burned down in 1930.

The Pentagon isn't in the District of Columbia, but rather Arlington, **Virginia**, which is why it has twice as many bathrooms as necessary. When the colossal edifice was built in the 1940s, Virginia still had segregation laws requiring separate toilet facilities for blacks and whites.

 Virginian Thomas Jefferson became comatose on July 2, 1826. On July 3 he awakened and asked, "Is it the Fourth?" He died 50 minutes into the next day — the 50th anniversary of the Declaration of Independence. He expired a few hours before his onetime rival and fellow president, John Adams. Adams' fond last words, "Thomas Jefferson still survives," were mistaken.

Ten years later, fourth President James Madison started to fade away. During his final illness in the summer of 1836, he refused the request of friends to take stimulants to prolong his life until July 4, the 60th anniversary of the Declaration of Independence. All were aware that Thomas Jefferson and John Adams had died on the 50th anniversary of the famous document. A few days before July 4th, Madison was found dead in his bedroom, sitting before his untouched breakfast tray.

The disappearance of England's first New World colony 420 years ago is surely America's oldest unsolved mystery. The puzzle of the Lost Colony still haunts Roanoke Island, **North Carolina**.

Backed by Sir Walter Raleigh and Queen Elizabeth I, a colony of 116 people arrived at Roanoke Island in 1587. Their transport ship returned to England with a promise to come back within three months. But war between England and Spain resulted in the confiscation of all ships for military purposes. Thus, re-supply was delayed for three years. In the meantime, baby Virginia Dare became the first English child born in the New World. When their ship at last returned in 1590, the colony had disappeared virtually without a trace. There was but one clue: the word "CROATON" carved into a tree.

A decade before the start of the Civil War, Goldsboro, **North Carolina** was the scene of one of America's most tragic and ironic events: A free black man named Wynne had purchased his wife's freedom from slavery, and together they established a home and started a family. When Wynne fell into debt, his wife and children were forcibly returned to slavery to satisfy the family debt. The law of the land allowed this because she and her offspring were considered personal property by the fact that he had originally purchased her freedom.

Like most other Native American tribes, the Tuscarora of the Carolinas were decimated by smallpox, an Old World disease for which they had no natural immunity. In many villages, 90% of inhabitants died gruesome deaths. In truth the European conquest of Native Americans was more a matter of smallpox than of battles won. There were even isolated cases of whites offering Indian tribes intentionally smallpox-infected blankets. Though most native people did not survive, many pieces of aboriginal wisdom have survived:

They are not dead who live in the hearts they leave behind. (Tuscarora)

Best to have less thunder in the mouth and more lightning in the hand. (Apache)

Before eating, always take time to thank the food. (Arapaho)

The frog does not drink up the pond in which he lives. (Lakota)

A brave man dies but once, a coward many times. (Tribe Unknown)

The weird zigzag in the North Carolina-**South Carolina** border near Charlotte dates from 1772. That's when boundary commissioners altered the line to avoid splitting the Catawba Indians between the two British colonies.

In 1802, the state of **Georgia** yielded its claims to lands in the western part of the state to the U.S. government. These lands later became Alabama and Mississippi. In exchange, Georgia expected the federal government to remove the Indian tribes, thus allowing the state of Georgia full control of its territory.

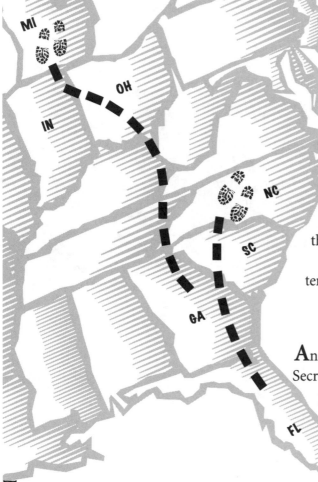

It may seem counter-intuitive, but the "Sunshine State" of **Florida** really should be called the "Partly Cloudy State," as it has more days where clouds block 20-70 percent of the sun than any other state. In fact, Florida doesn't even make the list of the five sunniest states. Here they are, starting with the sunniest: Arizona, California, Nevada, New Mexico, and Texas.

Florida's coastline is more than 2,200 miles long. In the United States as elsewhere, the three-mile limit is the traditional (though now largely obsolete) definition of a nation's territorial waters. This law of the seas was based on the distance that coastal cannons could effectively fire cannonballs.

Andrew Jackson appointed Stevens T. Mason as Secretary of **Michigan** Territory when Mason was just 19 years old. When Territorial Governor George Porter died in office, 22-year-old Mason became the so-called "Boy Governor," a nickname he detested.

The jerky driving habits of his lawyer inspired Hagerstown, **Indiana** inventor Ralph Teetor to imagine a solution. He was frustrated when his lawyer would slow down while talking and then speed up when listening. Teetor's resulting invention was cruise control, a device he patented in 1945. Teetor was blind, making him especially sensitive to the stop-and-go motion of cars.

It's not your usual pharmacy: The Penn-Ohio Medicine Mart straddles the state line of **Ohio** and Pennsylvania. A thick red line is painted on the floor so patrons always know in which state they're shopping. The store maintains two mailing addresses and two phones, one for each state. Because the store sells lottery tickets from two states, there are two lotto machines — each legally located in its proper state. When one or both state lotteries promise a high jackpot, the lines get so long that they cross into the adjoining state.

Shallow Buckeye Lake, east of Columbus, **Ohio**, formed in the last Ice Age. In 1826, Ohio began creating an elaborate canal system. Buckeye became a "feeder" lake required to keep the canals flowing. As water levels rose in the swampy lake, a nearly 50-acre chunk of cranberry-sphagnum broke loose from the bottom to form a spongy floating island! Today the island still floats and hikers wander on boardwalks among meadows and beneath sizable trees.

If you've ever failed to return a book to the library, or simply lost a book, this may make you feel better:

At the height of the Great Depression, Cleveland, **Ohio** hosted an unofficial world's fair. The sprawling Great Lakes Expo was visited by 7 million people. Each visitor was invited to sign what was then considered the world's largest book.

The so-called *Golden Book of Cleveland* was meant to preserve for posterity the names of fair visitors. It was seven feet tall, five feet wide and weighed nearly 2.5 tons. The massive book, all 6,000 pages, mysteriously disappeared after the expo closed, and hasn't been seen since.

It's said old soldiers never die, they just fade away. That was nearly the case with ol' John Gray. As a boy Gray joined his father as a day laborer for George Washington. Washington left to take command of the Continental Army when the Revolutionary War began, and the senior Gray joined him. When John's father was killed in battle, the 17-year-old enlisted to take his place. Gray subsequently saw action at the Battles of Williamsburg and Yorktown.

Gray moved to **Ohio,** then the western frontier. Though eligible for a pension as a Revolutionary War veteran, he was denied those funds by bureaucratic stumbling blocks until 1867, when a group of Civil War veterans took up Gray's cause. Congress finally approved his pension, but Gray was dead within a year. He was 104. The pension had been a respectable amount for that era: $49 a month.

The good folks of **Ohio** have a bone to pick with North Carolina. According to Ohioans, the Tarheels' claim as the "birthplace of aviation" is a stretch. Ohio residents Wilbur and Orville Wright designed, wind-tunnel tested and built the first airplane in Ohio, only to ship their "Flyer" to Kitty Hawk, North Carolina to attempt the inaugural flight in more favorable ocean winds.

It was at Kitty Hawk in 1903 that they made a couple of very short flights, none longer than one minute. The flying machine was underpowered and uncontrollable. The Wright brothers realized they had much to do to perfect their invention.

To truly learn to fly, the Wright brothers established the world's first test-flight facility at Ohio's Huffman Prairie. There they made flight after flight for two years and in the process fine-tuned the controls, engine, and propellers. At Kitty Hawk they could fly only a few feet off the ground, and only in a straight line. In **Ohio** they flew for more than half an hour or until their fuel ran out, and made controlled turns. The birthplace of flight: Ohio or North Carolina? You decide. Both jurisdictions celebrate the Wright Brothers "flyer" on their state quarters.

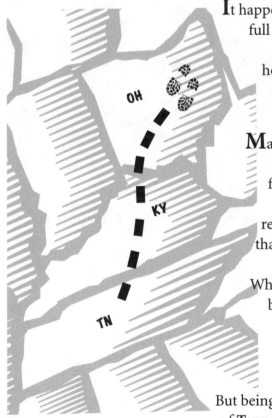

It happened in 1931 during baseball's golden era: Armed with full catcher's gear and an oversized mitt, Joe Sprinz of the Cleveland Indians caught a baseball dropped from a hovering dirigible 800 feet above. While he handled the ball neatly, the impact created a shock wave through his body that fractured poor Joe's jaw.

Margaret Garner escaped from slavery with her children. She hiked crossed **Kentucky** before reaching that freedom river, the Ohio. After successfully crossing the river into Cincinnati, Garner was about to be recaptured when she resolved to kill her children rather than condemn them to a life of slavery. She succeeded in killing her daughter, but her sons were only injured. When Garner stood trial, it was ironically not for murder but for the apparently greater crime of being a fugitive slave. The incident later was the basis for Toni Morrison's novel *Beloved*.

Americans set high standards for their presidents. But being human, they've all had their blemishes. Take the case of **Tennessee** native son Andrew Jackson. He married his wife, Rachel, before her divorce from her first husband was finalized. Scandalously, the future First Lady was married to two men at once for several weeks.

When Andrew Jackson ran for president, opponents sometimes twisted his name by calling him "jackass." Old Hickory, who relished controversy, liked the image so much that the jackass, or donkey, became the new symbol of his Democratic party.

President Andrew Johnson was a tailor who made all his own clothes until becoming a congressman. Though a Southerner who had held slaves, he was against the South's secession from the Union. This prompted many Southerners to consider him a traitor. While attempting to return home to **Tennessee** after Lincoln's inauguration, Johnson encountered a mob in Lynchburg, Virginia. They dragged Johnson from the train, beating, kicking and spitting on him. They were about to hang the future president when an old man shouted, "His neighbors at Greeneville have made arrangements to hang their senator on his arrival. Virginians have no right to deprive Tennessee of that privilege." When Tennessee seceded from the Union, Johnson was forced to flee his own state.

Have you ever wondered why legislative bills are read aloud? In early America many adults could not read and write — and that applied to lawmakers, too. No one wanted votes to be cast for legislation that hadn't been read, or at least heard. Borderline illiteracy extended even to these presidents from **Tennessee**: Andrew Jackson was a poor speller who said that anyone who spelled things the same way every time showed a lack of imagination. Andrew Johnson never attended school — he was taught to read as an adult by his wife.

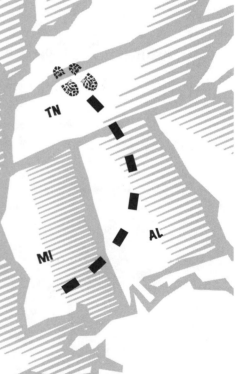

At one time or another, 40 states had laws forbidding the marriage of people of different races. When these laws were declared unconstitutional in 1967, many states nonetheless retained the statutes. In 2005, **Alabama** was the last to repeal the law.

The community of Selma, **Alabama** is best remembered as a flash point of the Civil Rights Movement. But it could also be remembered for resident Dr. Joshua Vick. Way back in the 1880s, druggist Lunsford Richardson concocted a salve for chest colds. Richardson eventually named it after his Selma-based brother-in-law. He called it Vicks VapoRub.

Mississippi's Pascagoula River makes a weird singing sound resembling a swarm of bees. Scientists theorize it may be the sound of sand scraping the river's hard bottom, or natural gas escaping from below. No cause has been proven. Pascagoula Indians said it was the sound of their ancestors who, realizing they couldn't win a battle with the Biloxi tribe, walked into the river singing their death song.

Mississippi's Dr. James Hardy is best remembered for a chimp-to-human heart transplant, but his groundbreaking lung transplant was equally controversial. The recipient, who suffered from failing pulmonary function, was a death-row inmate. Though scheduled for execution, the patient was told that in return for submitting to the experimental transplant, **Mississippi** authorities would consider a pardon based on his "… contribution to science and humanity." The inmate/patient died of complications, though the lung transplant likely prolonged his life.

During a University of **Minnesota** football game in 1898, student Johnny Campbell jumped in front of the home crowd and led an organized yell to become the nation's first cheerleader.

The search for the headwaters of the Mississippi River, much like the fabled quest for the source for the Nile, became a near-obsession for some folks. In 1805, Lt. Zebulon Pike was sent to explore the Mississippi's headwaters, and after much searching he incorrectly proclaimed Cass Lake as the river's source. Finally, in 1832, Henry Schoolcraft crowned several failed attempts by correctly determining the source as Lake Itasca. Modern visitors to Minnesota's Lake Itasca may quite literally jump across the Mississippi as it exits the lake.

Before statehood, **Wisconsin** was a land of often inadequate housing. Miners and their families sometimes lived in the mines in which they worked. When such miners were compared to badgers, the Badger State found its nickname.

Crippled and unable to fulfill his Civil War duty, Dan McCann of Chippewa Falls, Wisconsin, instead sent his pet eagle, Old Abe, because "…someone from the family ought to go." The eagle screamed encouragement to his regiment through 42 skirmishes and battles, and lost only a few feathers. The heroic bird was given to the state in 1864 and lived in Wisconsin's capitol building.

In 1903, Arthur Davidson and William Harley built their first motorcycle, a racing bike, in a **Milwaukee** shed. Harley-Davidson Corp. would go on to become one of America's top business success stories.

In 1870, the word "blizzard" as first used to describe a violent snowstorm in the *Vindicator* newspaper in tiny Estherville, **Iowa**. Midwestern newspapers subsequently popularized the usage. "Blizzard" originally described a volley of musket fire.

Each August the river towns of Le Claire, **Iowa** and Port Byron, Illinois, hold an old-fashioned tug-of-war with an odd twist: The 2,400-foot-long rope is stretched across the Mississippi River! It is the only recreational event sanctioned to stop traffic on the great river.

Southern **Illinois** is sometimes referred to as "Little Egypt." Settled by migrants from the South, it's culturally distinct from the rest of Illinois. Although Illinois was a free state prior to the Civil War, limited slavery was allowed in Little Egypt. In one example, the operator of a salt mine was permitted to own slaves because he found it impossible to hire wage earners for the fearsome work. His mine was near the ironically named berg of Equality, Illinois.

In 1881, **Illinois** native Charles Guiteau shot and mortally wounded President James Garfield. Or did he? During his murder trial Guiteau maintained that Garfield's incompetent doctors had actually killed the president, not he. Most historians now agree: Several doctors inserted their unsterilized fingers into the wound to probe for the bullet, and one doctor even punctured Garfield's liver in the process. The result was eventual death by blood poisoning.

In Bloomington **Illinois** in 1856, Abraham Lincoln delivered his "Lost Speech," a speech purportedly so compelling that reporters forgot to take notes...and therefore they could not reproduce the speech for newspapers and posterity.

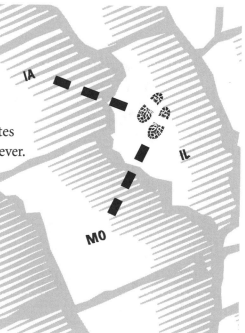

 Two years later, the Lincoln-Douglas debates gripped the nation like no campaign event ever. This was due partly to the telegraph, a brand-new technology that speedily delivered debate transcripts to newspapers nationwide. At one debate site in southern Illinois, Lincoln felt obligated to counter Douglas' qualified support for slavery by reminding voters that Abe himself wasn't advocating racial equality. The following words may seem unworthy of the author of the Gettysburg Address, yet they were indeed spoken by the same president who later freed the slaves:

"I am not nor have I ever been in favor of making voters or jurors of Negroes, nor of qualifying them to hold office, nor to intermarry with white people, and I will say in addition that there is a physical difference between white and black races which I believe will forever forbid the two races living together on terms of social and political equality... (and) while they do remain together there must be a position of superior and inferior, and I as much as any other man am in favor of having the superior position assigned to the white race."

Bloody Island was a wooded sandbar in the Mississippi River opposite St. Louis and a favorite rendezvous for dualists because it was considered exempt from the laws of either **Missouri** or Illinois. Here the "Dual of the Governors" was fought — one participant would later become

Missouri's Confederate governor, while the other became the state's "Union" governor after the Civil War.

Duals were fought only by gentlemen and never by commoners. Preservation of "honor" was often more important than killing the opponent. Yet duals could be deadly. Sitting Vice President Aaron Burr mortally wounded Alexander Hamilton. Button Gwinnett, a signer of the Declaration of Independence, died in a dual. Andrew Jackson killed one dueling adversary but suffered a chest wound that caused him a lifetime of pain. Henry Clay survived a dual, as did Abraham Lincoln. While still in Illinois, Lincoln had once been obligated to accept a dual challenge from state auditor James Shields. In an attempt to defuse the situation with humor, Lincoln's first choice of weapons was cow pies. Shields was only further insulted, so Lincoln reluctantly chose cavalry broadswords. Arriving early, Lincoln displayed his great height by hacking at the upper branches of a nearby tree. When Shields noted Abe's reach advantage, he called off the dual.

Missouri Senator David Rice Atchison was President of the United States for only one day. The term of James K. Polk ended at noon on March 4, 1849. Because this was a Sunday, the devout Zachary Taylor refused to be sworn in until the next day. Because Polk's vice president had resigned a few days earlier, by law the president pro tempore of the Senate automatically became president during the vacancy. That person was Atchison. He later said, "I slept most of that Sunday." His gravestone says, "President of U.S. one day."

The ample trapdoor of the Fort Smith, **Arkansas** gallows allowed Isaac "Hanging Judge" Parker to dispatch six or more condemned men simultaneously. When the gallows was dismantled in 1897, this broad trapdoor was "recycled" into a front porch for a modest nearby home. Bare-footed children playing on that porch could scarce imagine the grim footsteps of former years.

In the 1930s, Hot Springs, **Arkansas** was a refuge for gangsters and organized criminals. By unwritten decree, Hot Springs was where the bad guys vacationed and was thus off limits to any kind of criminal activity. Apparently two petty thieves didn't get the memo. After robbing a bank in downtown Hot Spring, their murdered bodies were found a few miles north on Route 7, still sitting in their Model T with the money on the seat between them.

America owes its largest purchase and arguably greatest bargain, the Louisiana Purchase, to a slave revolt in French Haiti. When French Emperor Napoleon spent heavily in a failed effort to put down the revolt, he felt compelled to sell the massive **Louisiana** Territory to fund his European war.

Louisiana's peculiar Voodoo religion contains superstitions such as the following: If a woman's husband dies and you don't want her to re-marry, cut all of her deceased husband's shoes into little pieces and she will never marry again. The New Orleans form of voodoo was influenced by Haitian vodou, which contains elements of African, European and Roman Catholic belief. In 1533, a Catholic priest in Haiti performed a roughshod autopsy on the bodies of two dead Siamese-twin children to determine whether they contained one or two souls. When he found two hearts, two stomachs, four lungs, etc., he determined there were two souls. However, the priest had a financial bias in the outcome. The controversy began when the infants' father balked at the idea of paying for two baptisms, claiming the twins were one body with just one soul.

Louisiana was one of a handful of pre-Civil War states where blacks could own slaves. One census revealed that 735 "free people of color" owned 2,351 slaves.

Early on the morning of Nov. 21, 1980, 12 men abandoned their oil drilling rig in the middle of Louisiana's Lake Peigneur, when their drill suddenly seized up at 1,230 feet below the muddy surface. Sensing something had gone terribly wrong, the men scrambled into a boat bound for shore. Soon they watched in amazement as the $5 million Texaco drilling platform disappeared into a lake that was thought to be just 11 feet deep. The water of the lake began to churn, steadily accelerating until it became a fast-moving whirlpool a quarter mile in diameter. It turns out the site's drill had inadvertently pierced the dome of a large underground salt mine. Miraculously, the 50 salt miners all escaped in elevators despite water pouring in from above. The lake was drained of its 3.5 billion gallons of water in just three hours. Then water began flowing *in* from the nearly Gulf of Mexico, forming a 150-foot waterfall into the crater where the lake had been!

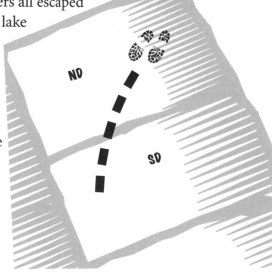

Mildly wacky fact: Twice **North Dakota** lawmen have unsuccessfully pushed to shorten the state's name to just "Dakota." Really wacky fact: If North Dakota seceded from the Union, it would instantly become the world's third largest nuclear power.

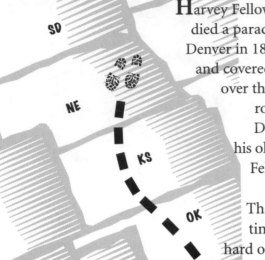

Harvey Fellows, Deadwood **South Dakota's** last stagecoach driver, died a paradoxical death. Having learned the stagecoach trade in Denver in 1863, he safely drove stagecoaches for a record 50 years and covered 300,000 miles. Fellows galloped the last stagecoach over the Deadwood-Spearfish Trail in 1913, a year when the road was upgraded for auto use. In 1929, organizers of Deadwood's Days of '76 asked Fellows to climb aboard his old coach as part of the parade. Feeble and nearly blind, Fellows agreed to ride if the stagecoach was placed on a flatbed truck. All went well until the parade ended. That's when Harvey alighted as he had done a thousand times — but this time he missed the flatbed and landed hard on the ground below. Harvey Fellows never recovered.

The world's greatest variance in temperature, according to *Guinness Book of Records*, belongs to **South Dakota's** Black Hills. It happened in 1943 when the thermometer stood at a frigid minus four degrees. That's when the temperature shot up 49 degrees in less than two minutes. So rapid was the temperature shift that plate glass windows cracked. Motorists crossing from the "ice box" zone to the warmer air mass were forced to pull over when a peculiar frost instantly obscured their windshields. In some locations the temperature gyrated like a rollercoaster. The Montana-Dakota Utilities printout thermometer rocketed from 9 degrees to 57 degrees and then back down to 10 degrees, all between 10:30 a.m. and 11:00 a.m.

In 1877, a flood on the Missouri River permanently separated the community of Carter Lake from the rest of Iowa and placed it on the **Nebraska** side of the big river — completely surrounded by Nebraska tuft. The U.S. Supreme Court ruled in 1892 that the town nevertheless belonged to Iowa. Still legally part of Council Bluffs, Iowa, Carter Lake residents lacked city services enjoyed by fellow residents across the river, but they were still subject to city taxes. The community defiantly seceded from Council Bluffs in the 1920s, and henceforth incorporated. To this day, travelers driving to Omaha's airport are surprised and confused by the "Welcome to Iowa" sign as they approach Eppley Field.

Kansas has surprising ties to Spanish conquestadors and Southwestern culture. Coronado Heights in east-central Kansas is allegedly the hill where Coronado finally gave up his quest for the fabled Seven Cities of Gold — an event just four decades after the voyages of Columbus. Then in 1692, following Spanish suppression of the Pueblo Revolt in present-day New Mexico, one band of Taos natives escaped Spanish dominion by fleeing far to the northeast. Near an eerie rock formation known as the Kansas Pyramids, they built adobe homes and irrigation systems in this most northerly of all pueblos, known as El Quartelejo.

During the infamous **Tulsa** Race Riots of 1921, authorities used military biplanes to discharge rifles and drop incendiary bombs on buildings, homes and fleeing African-American families.

The six planes were trainers left over from World War I, and were dispatched from nearby Curtis Field. What was at first described as a "Negro uprising" was determined to be a riot of mostly white Tulsans targeting the affluent black "Greenwood" neighborhood. By the time martial law was declared, an estimated 75-300 people were dead. Not all Tulsans shared the aims of the rioters. Some whites and Hispanics in neighborhoods adjacent to Greenwood took up arms in defense of their black neighbors.

Older history books taught that **Texans** fought Mexicans at the Alamo, suggesting the two armies were aligned by race rather than national loyalty. This over-simplification didn't help subsequent Anglo-Hispanic relations in Texas. The truth is more complex.

Take the case of Damacio Jimenez, unrecognized as an Alamo defender for 150 years. In 1986, lawyer Raul Casso IV was working among San Antonio's old government documents when he stumbled across a petition for a land grant from Jimenez's heirs. Their written rationale for the grant was simple: Damacio had died defending the Alamo, a fact previously unknown to historians.

The majority of the Alamo's famed defenders, such as Davy Crockett and Sam Bowie, were recent immigrants to Texas. But of the 11 native-born Texans martyred at the Alamo, nine had Spanish surnames.

Slave importation was made illegal in the United States in 1820. However, some Southern firebrands who promoted secession also strongly advocated reinstating the foreign slave trade. **Texan** Charles Lamar was a leading advocate. Lamar and co-conspirators purchased the yacht the *Wanderer*, sailing her to Africa in 1858 to bring back slaves. Lamer's crew dodged British and American naval vessels patrolling the coast of Africa, and safely returned to the United States with the human cargo.

Lamar and his colleagues evaded American justice through a combination of corruption and intimidation. In three separate trials in 1859, Lamar and his co-conspirators were each time acquitted despite the best efforts of the Buchanan administration to convict and execute them.

There was, however, this poetic justice: Lamar was killed in action during the Civil War. The *Wanderer* was seized by the U.S. government and ended up in the Union fleet during the war.

In the open range days before barbed wire, cowboys routinely branded cattle before turning them loose. A "maverick" was the term for a stray cow belonging to one ranch but found roaming with a herd bearing brands of another ranch. We owe the term to **Texas** rancher Samuel Maverick, who refused to brand his own stock as a way of claiming all unbranded stock was his!

History is written by the winners. But certain revisionists now refer to "The Myth of The Alamo," as a way of dismantling our romanticized version of the mission's defense. According to this new version, the defenders were a small group of pro-slavery Southerners and a handful of Mexican allies who were trying to subvert Mexico's anti-slavery laws. The Mexican government had outlawed slavery long before the United States, which meant slavery was banned in their northern frontier that today we call **Texas**.

Montana's Battle of the Little Big Horn is chock full of curiosities. Take the case of a Lakota named Good Fox. Though he wanted to participate in the Custer fight, gentle-spirited Good Fox wasn't a "killing man." Instead he showed his bravery by counting coup — zigzagging among the enemy and touching them with his crooked coup stick, which was wrapped in otter fur.

For the Lakota, counting coup was the practice of touching a living enemy. Counting coup was often considered a greater distinction than actually killing the enemy. Fourteen years after his exploits at the Little Big Horn, Good Fox survived the Wounded Knee massacre. He lived until 1928.

Certain Indian tribes venerated large carnivores in ways that seemed strange to Anglo-Americans, such as this adage of the Blackfoot Indians: "The gun that fires on a wolf or coyote will never again shoot straight."

During the Great Depression, a half-serious attempt was made to create a new state of Absaroka. A governor was appointed, and Sheridan, **Wyoming**, was declared the capital. The "state" boundaries were to have been the northern third of Wyoming, the western third of South Dakota and southeastern Montana. This was a region that felt its ranching way of life was being ignored by federal relief efforts. Absaroka even issued car license plates, crowned a Miss Absaroka of 1939 and hosted a state visit from the King of Norway.

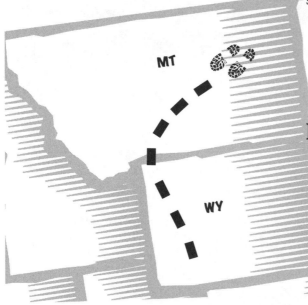

In the old days Meeteetse, **Wyoming** had a bank. Late one July afternoon, business was slow and the day was picture perfect, which meant the bank manager couldn't resist the temptation to grab his rod and walk to nearby Greybull River for a little fly fishing. A short time later the state bank inspector happened to arrive from distant Cheyenne, only to find the front door open and the bank empty. The inspector was extremely unhappy, and to teach the absent bank manager a lesson he reached over the counter and pushed the alarm button. Promptly the waitress from the Outlaw Bar showed up, with two beers on a tray!

In 1960, an early warning radar system alerted NORAD headquarters in **Colorado** of a massive Soviet nuclear missile strike approaching the United States. Actually it was the fault of a computer that removed two zeros from the warning system's ranging components. This caused the radar to detect a supposed missile attack 2,500 miles away, but in fact the radar had detected a reflection of the moon, located 250,000 miles away!

A huge stand of aspen trees on Kebler Pass in **Colorado** is thought by some biologists to be the world's largest single organism. Because aspens propagate by sprouting from a common root system, the thousands upon thousands of interconnected aspens of the Kebler Pass grove do indeed share identical genetics. Each fall, the individual trees of this vast stand turn exactly the same shade of yellow/orange at precisely the same time. Aspens might also be considered the oldest living organisms. That's because while individual trees are short-lived, according to botanists A. Mackinnon and L. Kershaw an entire cloned grove could easily live for tens of thousands of years, or possibly even a million years!

The nation's oldest licensed pilot, 105-year-old Cole Kugel of Longmont, **Colorado**, died in June 2007. Less than two months before his death, Kugel had taken the controls of a small airplane on a flight between Longmont and Denver.

 **T**he Wild West's most heroic defense against the odds wasn't by a familiar figure such as Bill Hickok or Wyatt Earp. The title goes to a forgotten Hispanic deputy sheriff named Elfego Baca. In 1884, Baca volunteered to disperse a gang of unruly cowboys shooting up the one-horse town of Frisco, **New Mexico** Territory. What he didn't expect to find was 80 heavily armed and ill-tempered cowpokes that eventually cornered Baca in a tiny adobe hut.

For 38 hours, Baca's 80 assailants fired an estimated 4,000 rounds in his direction. When finally rescued by fellow lawmen, Baca had survived without a scratch — and by some accounts had managed to kill four of his assailants while wounding eight others. The door to the besieged adobe hut contained 367 bullet holes!

When the Lewis and Clark Expedition crossed the Continental Divide at Lemhi Pass in present-day **Idaho**, they were by some definitions trespassing on foreign territory — U.S. soil as defined by the Louisiana Purchase ended at the Divide. Americans sometimes forget that Lewis and Clark weren't the first whites to make a transcontinental crossing of North America. They were beaten to the punch by 11 years when Canadian Alexander Mackenzie crossed the mountains of that nation to reach the Pacific. Alas, Mackenzie would have been an American, but his Scottish-born parents were Tories who fled New York for Montreal at the onset of the American Revolution.

When early explorers stood on the shores of **Utah's** Great Salt Lake, they noted the salty taste, and couldn't see across the waters. Naturally they assumed they had found a bay of the Pacific Ocean.

When completed in 1935, Hoover Dam on the **Arizona-Nevada** border was the world's largest electric power producing facility and the world's largest concrete structure.

There were 112 deaths associated with the dam's construction. The first person to die was J. G. Tierney, a surveyor who drowned while looking for an ideal spot for the dam. In an eerie coincidence, his son Patrick W. Tierney was the last man to die working on the dam, 13 years to the day later.

Arizona law once prohibited persons of "mixed race" from marrying anyone, even each other!

Shhhh! Acoustic ecologist Gordon Hempton has found what may be the nation's quietest place: the Hoh Rain Forest of Olympic National Park, west of **Seattle**. Marked by a small red stone and the designation "one square inch of silence," the spot preserves a location where manmade sounds such as airplane engines generally can't be heard.

When a pig belonging to Englishman Charles Griffin was found rooting in American settler Lyman Cutlar's garden on San Juan Island (territory that both the United States and Great

Britain claimed), Cutlar shot it. This event in 1859 launched the so-called "Pig War," which was finally settled in 1872 in favor of the United States. The pig was the only casualty.

In 1952, black actor/singer Paul Robeson performed at Peace Arch Park in Blaine, **Washington**. He had been invited to perform in Canada, but the State Department revoked his passport and denied him permission to leave the country because he was a suspected Communist. In response, Robeson set up a stage, facing Canada, on a flatbed truck parked one foot from the border. There he performed for a crowd of 40,000 Americans and Canadians.

D.B. Cooper hijacked a Northwest Airlines plane en route to Seattle on Nov. 24, 1971. After the plane refueled in Seattle, and Cooper received a $200,000 ransom, he ordered the plane's crew to fly to Mexico. Near the town of Ariel, **Washington**, he parachuted from the plane and was never seen again. Ariel commemorates the mystery each year with a party.

The border between Canada and the United States runs straight as an arrow along the 49th parallel, and works just fine until the line reaches ocean waters south of Vancouver, where it cuts off a tiny piece of what should be Canada and assigns it instead to the state of **Washington**. This odd piece of America hanging out in the Pacific is Point Roberts. Old-timers suggested this wacky appendage should be handed back to Canada. On the bright side, the tiny five-square-mile enclave is virtually crime free, thanks to icy waters on three sides and border agents patroling the north side of town. The downside is it's a long drive through Canada when one of Point Roberts' 1,300 residents wants to see an American doctor, fill a prescription or buy a license plate.

In certain years on **Oregon's** central coast, significant winter storms will scour the beaches to reveal some strange sights: Lower sand levels expose the ancient "ghost forest" stumps on beaches just north of Newport. During these rare times you can see the stumps at Beverly Beach, at Moolack and further south at Beaver Creek. Perhaps 5,000 years old or older, these are the reminders of a massive earthquake on the Oregon coast that dropped an entire section of forest into the surf, where the normal decay is greatly slowed by the salt water.

In 1977, during an Eastern Oregon roundup of wild horses, the Bureau of Land Management (BLM) staff noticed some animals shared striking and primitive markings — zebra-like stripes on the upper legs and shoulders, and a black mark down the middle of the back known as a dorsal stripe. These were the last of the Kiger Mustangs, descendents of purebred Spanish horses brought to the New World in the 16th century. The BLM agreed to preserve the breed by releasing all 27 surviving Kigers into two highly remote areas of Oregon where interbreeding with other wild horses would be unlikely.

The odd moving stones of Death Valley, **California's** Racetrack Playa are a "win" for those who maintain that science can't solve every mystery. We know from trails left in the dry mud of this perfectly flat lakebed that such stones move in strange zigzag and looping paths. The roving stones vary from pebble-size up to a half-ton. The prevailing scientific explanation is that high winds move the rocks when icy rains make the mud slippery. This explanation fails to explain why a larger stone will move, while a smaller stone beside it fails to budge. Death Valley Monument Superintendent Don Spalking sums it up: "The experts have been coming here for years, but no one has actually seen a stone move. We know they do move, but we don't know how or why."

San Francisco is the gay capital of America, but that wasn't always the case. In the 19th and early 20th centuries the city hosted a quiet and slowly declining homosexual population. During World War II, military regulations against homosexuals meant that alleged gay soldiers and sailors serving their country in the Pacific theater were kicked out of the service and shipped to San Francisco for dishonorable discharge. Many of those discharged felt they couldn't return to their hometowns, so thousands made a new home in the City by the Bay's suddenly burgeoning gay community.

Alaska's Denali, also known as Mount McKinley, is easily North America's highest mountain at 20,320 feet. When approached from the south, the colossus rises 18,000 feet in just 12 miles. This is a greater vertical relief than Mount Everest. Due to the elevation gain and the mountain's sub arctic location, Denali is sometimes called the greatest climb in the world.

AK

Hawaii is the most isolated population center on Earth. The state is 2,390 miles from California, 3,850 miles from Japan, 4,900 miles from China and 5,280 miles from the Philippines.

Mount Everest may be the highest point on Earth, but by some definitions it's NOT the world's tallest mountain. That honor goes to Mauna Kea on the big island of Hawaii. Were the oceans to be drained, one could see that the submerged base of 13,681-foot Mauna Kea is actually 5.6 miles, or 30,000+ feet, below its summit.

HI

Visit www.StrangeTrueUS.com to discover free unpublished tales!

INDEX

Note: Each main state tale is bold-faced.